D1051939

PEACE,
WAR,
and
LIBERTY

Libertarianism
.org

PEACE, WAR, *and* LIBERTY

Understanding U.S. Foreign Policy

CHRISTOPHER A. PREBLE

Libertarianism
.org

Copyright ©2019 by the Cato Institute.
All rights reserved.

Print ISBN: 978-1-948647-16-8
eBook ISBN: 978-1-948647-17-5

Library of Congress Cataloging-in-Publication Data available.

Cover design: Charles Brock, Faceout Studio.
Interior design: TIPS Technical Publishing, Inc.

Printed in Canada.

Cato Institute
1000 Massachusetts Avenue, N.W.
Washington, D.C. 20001
www.cato.org

*To the scholars and staff of the Cato Institute,
and to our generous supporters*

Contents

Preface

This is a short book about a big topic: foreign policy. In the widest sense, a particular country's foreign policy pertains to the myriad ways in which that country's people engage and interact with people and institutions from other countries. The book focuses mainly on a particular class of people who have a particular responsibility for conducting a given country's foreign policy—chiefly its elected officials, military personnel, and diplomats. These people establish and enforce the rules governing how the rest of their country's people may or may not engage or interact with foreigners.

Some of these laws are fairly innocuous and impose only minor or temporary inconveniences. For example, U.S. law prohibits me from purchasing or owning certain items covered by U.S. sanctions. If I'm caught breaking the law, I could be prosecuted.

Collectively, the drafting and enforcing of such regulations necessitates a large and relatively intrusive state—larger, say, than a state that allowed me to purchase any good or service, from any place, regardless of the circumstances of its production or provision.

But war, that most visible of all instruments of foreign policy, imposes major and oftentimes lasting effects on individuals' lives and liberty.

War today is often seen as a foreign policy failure, but it wasn't always that way. The famed Prussian military theorist Carl von

Clausewitz described war as the continuation of policy by other means. Even militarily strong countries, however, would generally prefer to attain peacefully what *could* be secured by force. The reasons are fairly obvious and straightforward: War is unpredictable. War is costly. War is violent. Policymakers, therefore, should not embark on such a course lightly or with unrealistic expectations about quick success. Clausewitz spoke of friction, the fog of war, and how battle plans rarely survive first contact with the enemy. Winston Churchill, a celebrated wartime leader, was similarly mindful of war's uncertainty. "The Statesman who yields to war fever," he wrote in his memoir, *My Early Life*, "is no longer the master of policy, but the slave of unforeseeable and uncontrollable events."[1]

The liberals of Clausewitz's day, whom today we might call libertarians, had still more reasons for wanting to solve international problems by peaceful means. They knew that war often contributed to the rise of state power and therefore constituted a threat to liberty.

This book approaches warfare as they did: as an occasionally necessary evil, not an endeavor that should be used as a vehicle for promoting social change. The book is organized around a theory—or, more accurately, a set of different theories—about what best creates security and prosperity.

Simply, what causes peace? And relatedly, what can we do to advance individual liberty through peaceful means? In what instances, if any, is war the appropriate recourse? And what foreign policies other than war are more effective? This book addresses these questions.

Because I am an American, writing chiefly for an American audience, I will focus mostly on U.S. foreign policy. I believe that America's founding generation, in particular, proposed a foreign policy broadly consistent with libertarian principles, favoring peaceful engagement through trade and cultural exchange and holding a skepticism of warfare as an instrument of policy. Despite this U.S.-centric approach, I believe that the book has insights for many people in many countries. Identifying the particular pathologies that have afflicted U.S. foreign policy over time—foolish wars fought well, noble wars fought badly, well-intentioned restrictions on travel or trade that had unfortunate side effects, alliances created or dissolved—surely has relevance for other countries at other times.

The claim that U.S. foreign policy is like that of any other country comes with a crucial proviso: U.S. foreign policy is *bigger*—a function of our great wealth and power. The scope of any one nation's foreign policies is shaped by that nation's physical context, including its geography, and by the disposition (i.e., friend or foe) of its neighbors. Scope is also constrained by a given country's economic capacity to engage in all aspects of foreign policy—from conducting diplomacy to waging war.

Relatively small, relatively weak, or relatively poor countries must necessarily prioritize what they do. Medium- and large-sized countries also set priorities but can have more of them. Even relatively affluent countries often choose to privilege one aspect of foreign policy (e.g., trade) over another (e.g., war). Iceland's defense budget is effectively zero, as is Costa Rica's. The United States began as a small, weak country. Its constitution forbade a standing army, and it struggled in its early days to deploy forces even into neighboring Canada or Mexico. Today, the United States possesses the world's most powerful military. That vast force is capable of deploying in many places simultaneously and even performs many of the jobs that other countries assign solely to their diplomats.

This book proceeds in two parts. The first half explores the correlation between liberty and peace on the one hand, and illiberalism and war on the other, over the course of the last several hundred years. It begins by exploring how ideas about individual freedom—and the role that wars have played in advancing or impeding those ideas—evolved over time. It pays particular attention to the American experience, including especially the views of the Founders of the American republic, men such as George Washington, James Madison, and Thomas Jefferson, and their contemporaries and successors in the 18th and 19th centuries.

The American Founders had a clear vision for foreign policy. They established a set of criteria regarding foreign affairs, and fashioned a limited state to implement them. Those limits endured for more than a century. They advised against an ambitious and adventurous policy overseas that would necessitate large armies and navies—and a large state to support them. They believed that the costs and risks that such a state would pose to liberty were simply too great and that, from a practical perspective, the new nation was simply too small and weak to have much of an impact globally. They weren't merely limited by their circumstances, however; they also consciously constrained their own power. They hoped to fashion a *Novus Ordo Seclorum* ("A New Order of the Ages"). They objected to the very principle of empire practiced by the kings and princes that came before them. The United States, they explained, would be different.

Part I, then, traces the seemingly inexorable transformation of U.S. foreign policy in the 20th century from that espoused by the American Founders to one constructed around the growth of the state, creeping militarism, and frequent wars. Dwight David Eisenhower, though he made a career in the U.S. Army, lamented how the military-industrial complex threatened to permanently change the nature of the country that he led and served. In one of the first speeches of his presidency, delivered in March 1953, Eisenhower explained that the United States had, of necessity, adopted a semipermanent war footing. By the time of his farewell address, delivered nearly eight years later in January 1961, Eisenhower worried that it might never be rolled back.

Over 50 years later, Eisenhower's worst fears appear to have been realized. The armaments industry, which grew in order to contain and ultimately defeat the Soviet Union, remains largely intact nearly 30 years after that decrepit empire was consigned to the ash heap of history. The means to wage permanent war persist; the rationales have changed. After the end of the Cold War, and especially after the terrorist attacks on September 11, 2001, a military once geared to fight formidable states with modern arms was repurposed to fix weak states and to fight individuals formally attached to no state at all. It might later shift back to fight wars at sea against a modern state with a modern navy or to fight in the skies and space above.

Part II of the book moves from the past to the present, focusing on contemporary foreign policy debates. Specifically, it will scrutinize the wisdom or folly of particular approaches to foreign policy that modern policymakers and scholars employ on a regular basis. It offers a set of considerations to guide the evaluation of different foreign policy options, rather than specific recommendations for what should or should not be done. It explains why permanent, peacetime alliances can be a cause of war and why small, weak allies tend to free ride on their large, strong alliance partners. It doesn't set out to answer whether Ukraine should be a member of NATO or what Latvia should spend for its defense. This guide suggests why preventive wars—to change regimes or to denude a particular regime of its offensive weapons—have generally failed to achieve their objectives at a reasonable cost. It doesn't explain why, or whether, it would be foolish or wise for the United States to launch preventive wars against a nuclear-armed Pakistan or North Korea or China.

On balance, the book suggests questions to ask, but it does not pretend to know all the answers. Some of it is informed by libertarianism and reflects my healthy skepticism of the state. Other observations draw from history, the behavior of states, and the contexts and constraints in which they operate, but these observations are not connected to any particular political ideology. The primary object here is to help you gain a new appreciation for foreign policy's complexities and to introduce a set of criteria and considerations to keep in mind when evaluating it.

1

Introduction:
War Is the Health
of the State

Human liberty is the foundation of a good and just society. Men and women flourish when they are able to live, work, and play where they desire. People live better, more fulfilling lives when they are free to associate with the people they choose, and how they choose. The presumption of liberty, against the use of force to coerce or compel a person to behave in a particular way, defines the modern philosophy known today as libertarianism or, in an earlier era, liberalism.

Legitimate governments possess limited and enumerated powers to defend and protect basic human rights on behalf of their citizens. Governments provide a system for adjudicating disputes, and they impose sanctions or punishments on those who would transgress the rights of others either willfully or through negligence. Governments should adhere to the powers granted to them and otherwise interfere as little as possible with their citizens'

1

ability to make honest livings and enjoy the fruits of their labors. In domestic affairs, therefore, libertarians believe that the best governments are small governments.

The same principle of limited and enumerated powers applies when a government turns its attention abroad. People should generally be able to buy or sell goods or services, to study and travel, and to otherwise interact with others in a foreign country unencumbered by the intrusions of government. In other words, as a general rule, libertarians believe in the free movement of people and goods across borders and artificial boundaries that are often no more than lines on a map.

But a country's foreign policy goes well beyond what its government allows its citizens to do. Governments can choose to have formal relationships with other governments and peoples through diplomacy and the exchange of ambassadors. These agents, acting on behalf of a government and representing the interests of its constituents, may negotiate treaties of friendship or ones governing the terms of trade. Such activities are wise and just to the extent that they facilitate the individual's ability to live freely and prosper, both inside and outside the country in which he or she resides or was born.

Libertarians are skeptical, however, of government actions that depart from this narrow and well-defined mandate. Take, for example, the case of foreign aid—when a government provides direct financial assistance to a foreign government or people. Humanitarian assistance, especially in response to natural disasters, enjoys relatively broad support, even among some libertarians. But undemocratic governments can use foreign assistance—especially the military kind—to quell popular dissent. Some people, not just libertarians, may bristle at the idea that their government might tax them in order to provide public goods such as schools, roads, and bridges in a foreign land because the government there is unable or unwilling to do so. By contrast, few would object to nongovernmental entities performing similar services based on voluntary contributions of time or resources. After all, the ability of individuals to interact freely, including mutually beneficial trade and private charity, is a basic human right cherished by libertarians and nonlibertarians alike.

But while trade and other forms of voluntary engagement are essential elements of a country's foreign policy, war remains the most significant. Defense against threats, foreign and domestic, is one of the main reasons governments exist in the first place. While we should not define a country's foreign policy solely by the wars that it does or does not fight, the decisions on whether to initiate a war, or to engage in certain acts that may lead to war, are among the most important that a country and its leaders make. And while most people abhor war, libertarians have always had special reasons for doing so because of the unique threat that wars pose to liberty, including the loss of life and property.

A further reason libertarians fear war is because war grows the power of the state. As James Madison explained, "War is the parent of armies; from these proceed debts and taxes; and armies, and debts, and taxes are the known instruments for bringing the many under the domination of the few."[1]

Wars impede the free movement of goods, capital, and labor. Restrictions on such exchanges constitute an assault on fundamental human rights. And governments regularly abridge other rights during wartime in the service of a purportedly higher purpose. A government at war confiscates resources, undermining and circumventing the market with a degree of regimentation and central planning that would never be tolerated in peacetime.

War is the largest and most far-reaching of all government-run enterprises, and citizens' views of the state subtly but perceptively shift during wartime. "Individualism . . . flourishes during peacetime," explains Ronald Hamowy in *The Encyclopedia of Libertarianism*, "but clashes with the collectivism, regimentation, and herd mentality that war fosters."[2] Citizens who would typically demand an explicit justification for a particular government action grow quiescent during times of war. Those in uniform are bound by honor and law to obey the state's orders, as conveyed by the chain of command.

Civilians back on the home front are reluctant to go against authority for other reasons. War often brings violence, or the threat of violence, against dissenters. The safer course is to go along. And the social stigma of opposing a war, or the measures instituted to prosecute it, is also burdensome. Dissent can appear greedy or self-interested when one's fellow citizens are making heroic sacrifices. It seems particularly petty to complain that your taxes are too high, or that certain foods are less available, to a neighbor who has lost a son or daughter in combat. Your own sacrifices and privations pale in comparison.

In his sweeping survey, *War and the Rise of the State*, Bruce Porter summarizes the problem:

A government at war is a juggernaut of centralization determined to crush any internal opposition that impedes the mobilization of militarily vital resources. This centralizing tendency of war has made the rise of the state throughout much of history a disaster for human liberty and rights.[3]

Classical liberals jealously protect the rights of the individual and are committed to limiting the arbitrary powers of the state. Unsurprisingly, they are nearly unanimous in their opposition to war. Their ideology, Hamowy explains, looks "at war as a reactionary undertaking at odds with the social progress that springs, in large part, from the unhampered movement of goods, capital, and labor across national borders, and from international and scientific cooperation."[4] Adam Smith taught that "peace, easy taxes and a tolerable administration of justice"[5] were the essential ingredients of good government. Others excoriated war as inconsistent with social progress. A classical liberal, according to Ludwig von Mises, "is convinced that victorious war is an evil even for the victor, that peace is always better than war."[6]

About a year before his death, Nobel Laureate Milton Friedman warned that progress toward his goal of rolling back the federal government's power was being thwarted by the United States' overly ambitious and costly foreign policy. This included the idea that the United States had "a mission to promote democracy around the world." Friedman told the *San Francisco Chronicle*, "War is a friend of the state." It is always expensive, requiring higher taxes, and "in time of war, government will take powers and do things that it would not ordinarily do."[7]

The evidence is irrefutable: throughout human history, government has grown during wartime or during periods of great anxiety when war is in the offing, and it rarely surrenders these powers when the guns fall silent or when the crisis abates. Some instances are seemingly small but have far-reaching consequences. The first income tax in the United States was imposed during the Civil War. The first estate tax was collected to pay for the Spanish–American War. And the U.S. government implemented federal income tax withholding during World War II, increasing dramatically the government's ability to raise revenue while obscuring the true costs of government for most workers.

Other seemingly innocuous taxes or regulations linger long after their stated purposes with no good effect. The tax on long-distance telephone calls imposed to pay for the Spanish–American War lasted 108 years; the war lasted six months. Major American cities imposed rent controls during World War II, and some of these restrictions remain in place, most notably in New York City. Bruce Porter notes "the nonmilitary sectors of the federal government actually grew at a faster rate during World War II than under the impetus of the New Deal."[8] In other words, all aspects of state power expand during times of war, including those that have nothing to do with actually fighting and winning battles. The essential *Crisis and Leviathan* by the libertarian scholar Robert Higgs documents the phenomenon in great detail.[9] The litany of government abuses and usurpations that originated during wartime and persist to this day includes federal regulation of marriages, wage and price controls, the Internal Revenue Service, distortion of the health care market, inflation, bank bailouts, and morality crusades against alcohol and prostitution.[10]

It is demonstrably true that the state's power grows during wartime. War therefore always has the potential to undermine individual liberty, especially in the near term. It might be true that on balance, preparing for war in order to deter war, or waging a war now to prevent a worse one later, serves the cause of liberty and human rights. World War II falls into that category, given the unspeakable horror committed by Hitler's Germany in occupied Europe. (Imperial Japan's conduct in the Asia-Pacific, especially in China, was nearly as bad.) It seems clear in retrospect that war, and war alone, was necessary to stop those aggressors.

But ascertaining ahead of time that war is the last best hope for preserving liberty is always difficult, and it may be impossible. One country's preventive action may look like mere aggression to a disinterested third party. That is why the German statesman Otto von Bismarck is reported to have likened preventive war to committing "suicide from fear of death."[11]

Such counsel notwithstanding, the impulse to act is strong, especially when a nation possesses the capacity to do so. The ability to act, however, does not imply the ability to succeed. Mindful as we are that the road to hell is paved with good intentions, we must assess our actions by the tangible results delivered. And we should also attempt to ascertain whether comparable ends might have been achieved at less cost in blood and treasure. If a war was truly intended to advance the cause of human rights but resulted in millions of deaths, can we judge it a just and noble enterprise?

Only if we can be certain—and we rarely can be—that the alternative of inaction would have been far worse.

This bias against preventive action is consistent with classical liberal and libertarian ideas about the state's propensity to fail. Governments struggle to manage the domestic market or to deliver happiness to citizens close at hand. They struggle even more when attempting to manage far-off economies or distant peoples. And our skepticism should grow when their exertions rely on the use of force.

These doubts about the government's ability to produce noble ends by violence are informed by F. A. Hayek's observations on the "fatal conceit": the erroneous belief that "man is able to shape the world around him according to his wishes."[12] Hayek was particularly concerned about the problem of limited knowledge. He convincingly argued that government is incapable over the long term of regulating the economy or producing many public goods. Whereas the market relies on countless individuals pursuing their self-interest, no single human being can know all the tastes and preferences of his fellow citizens. Predicting their future desires is even harder.

The knowledge problem contributes to government's actions having unintended consequences, which can be serious enough in a domestic context. They are even more serious still in foreign policy. This is obvious when one recalls the banal point that wars kill and maim people and damage or destroy property. We can imagine many types of well-intentioned wars—for example, those aimed at advancing the cause of human rights and individual liberty by deposing an authoritarian tyrant. Still other "noble" wars may aim to correct a clear injustice—say, to reverse an aggressor's seizure of contested land in a neighboring sovereign state. Regardless of a belligerent's motivations, however, all wars unleash chaos and violence that cannot be limited solely to those deserving of punishment. And when the costs are finally tallied— to include not merely the lives lost, the property destroyed, and the vast expense incurred during the fighting, but also the costs of caring for the wounded, widowed, and orphaned—they almost always exceed the war hawks' confident predictions of quick and easy victory.

For all these reasons—the expansion of state power and the concomitant stifling of individual liberty on the home front, the problem of imperfect knowledge, and the unintended consequences visited upon the places where wars are fought—libertarians treat war for what it is: a sometimes necessary evil. "War cannot be avoided at all costs, but it should be avoided wherever possible," writes Cato's David Boaz in *The Libertarian Mind*. "Proposals to involve the United States—or any government—in foreign conflict should be treated with great skepticism."[13] The good and noble end of securing and advancing human liberty should, wherever possible, be achieved by peaceful means.

What might those be? And can liberty survive and thrive in the absence of a dominant liberal power like the United States?

Many people are skeptical. Liberty needs a champion, they say, particularly given the onslaught of illiberal movements and nation-states bent on thwarting freedom. The United States, they say, performs this service. "The most important features in today's world," writes the Brookings Institution's Robert Kagan, "the great spread of democracy, the prosperity, the prolonged great-power peace—have depended directly and indirectly on power and influence exercised by the United States."[14] That work must continue, Kagan and others argue. People living under a tyrant's heel must be liberated. Communities threatened by murderous gangs must be protected. The power of the U.S. military might be able to depose an authoritarian ruler, and it is certainly sufficient to kill or capture a band of ragtag thugs.

There has long been discussion about the United States performing this role, even before it had the military power to do so. George Washington in his Farewell Address and Thomas Jefferson in his first inaugural address advised their countrymen to steer clear of the internal affairs of foreign countries, and both were anxious for the United States to stay out of unnecessary foreign wars. But that did not imply a lack of concern for what happened beyond the new nation's borders. They and others in their generation hoped that the United States would serve as an example to the rest of the world, a successful experiment in individual liberty and limited government that others would want to emulate.

But maintaining this liberal order would be difficult, and it was always threatened by the prospect of foreign wars—especially by such wars' tendency to grow the power of the state. Efforts to spread liberty abroad could just as easily destroy it at home.

Such sentiments are less prevalent today. To the extent that they are even aware of the Founders' foreign policy views, many Americans consider them horribly antiquated. A few others see them as dangerously naive. Of course the United States has been a champion for liberty, they say, and not merely here at home. Just look at the nations liberated from fascism and communism in the 20th century. What would have happened if the United States had refrained from going abroad in World War II? How would the freedom and independence of Western Europe have fared absent U.S. conduct during the Cold War? Would South Korea or Taiwan have survived to become vibrant, prosperous democracies were it not for the heroic sacrifices that Americans made, and were prepared to make, to defend them?

It is reasonable to surmise that the epic contests of the mid-20th century would have ended differently were it not for U.S. involvement, and the result would almost certainly have been a setback for liberty. Meanwhile, the very different experiences to the east and west of the iron curtain in Europe after World War II remind us that the one-time U.S. ally against Nazi Germany was no friend of human rights. The Soviet occupation of postwar Eastern Europe might have permanently extinguished freedom's flame there. The U.S. government's policies during the Cold War, including the presence of many tens of thousands of U.S. troops in Western Europe, helped prevent that from happening.

But other factors contributed, too. While the U.S. military deterred overt Soviet aggression, American culture helped pry open societies that the Soviets and their cronies tried desperately to keep shut. Some of this cultural exchange was sponsored by the U.S. government, but most of it was not. Government-sponsored radio stations played Elvis Presley and the Beatles in the 1960s and 1970s, but Uncle Sam didn't produce rock-and-roll records. He didn't sell Levi's, and he didn't create Mickey Mouse. And while American weapons deterred Soviet actions, the nonbinding

Helsinki Accords, adopted by 35 countries in 1975 to reduce tensions and improve communication between East and West, may have done as much to break Moscow's control over the Warsaw Pact countries as Pershing missiles or the Strategic Defense Initiative.

Today, the Soviet Union is no more, and former Soviet client states have often been at the forefront of political and economic change in Eastern Europe. Indeed, freedom has *many* champions. These include countless libertarian foundations and nongovernmental organizations (NGOs) that promote basic concepts of liberty without relying on American taxpayers to fund their operations. These genuinely *non*governmental organizations (as opposed to quasigovernmental ones) do not act at the behest of the U.S. government; they do not follow orders from the Pentagon or its several combatant commanders. It is a disservice to the work of these organizations and individuals, and the ideas they promote, to suggest that they would fail and that these ideas would die were it not for the U.S. military. Liberty exists, after all, in places where U.S. soldiers have never set foot.

The real question, therefore, isn't *whether* we should wish to see freedom spread worldwide, but rather *how* it will spread. Some may call for wars of liberation or for diplomatic or economic pressure backed up by the threat of force in order to bring about regime change, be it in Iraq, Iran, Libya, Syria, Cuba, or North Korea. But these calls risk ignoring the harmful effects that these policies will have, and have had, on the people we are ostensibly attempting to free. It is reasonable for many Iraqis, Iranians, Libyans, Syrians, Cubans, or North Koreans to doubt that the United

States has brought them increased liberty, safety, or prosperity in the last quarter century.

Those who would proactively wage war, or threaten to do so, to liberate unfree people tend to ignore the enormous gains that freedom has made during the past half century that were achieved by entirely nonviolent means. People who are skeptical of the U.S. government's ability to deliver mail in the United States should be even more skeptical of that same government's ability to deliver democracy and good governance all around the world. Thankfully, many people around the world now work to spread the gospel of liberty, and those who are most successful do their work voluntarily and promote their ideas peacefully.

Indeed, in many ways, peace is the essence of libertarianism. An international order that was less dependent upon U.S. military power as a vehicle for promoting liberty—one that was based instead on the presumption that all governments have a core obligation to defend the rights and liberties of their citizens and to advance their security—could be a safer one. It could also be a freer one.

Human beings are generally reluctant to go to war, and more so now than 70 or 500 years ago. Harvard's Steven Pinker has documented the dramatic decline in all forms of violence committed by humans against other humans.[15] But that doesn't mean that violence has disappeared or that it ever will. A basic survival instinct leads us to believe in self-defense when our physical security is threatened, for example. And individuals sometimes initiate violence when they sense that a proximate danger will only become more urgent in the future. It is unreasonable to ask a man to suffer the first blow in a fistfight or to wait until *after* members of his family are assaulted or killed before retaliating against the perpetrators.

Governments, too, sometimes initiate wars. But to do so other than in those rare instances when all other options have been exhausted would be irresponsible. Wars—all wars—are costly and risky enterprises. Hawks, those men and women most inclined to support the use of force, don't dispute that fact, but they do tend to downplay the dangers while playing up the possible benefits. The rest of us should retain our skepticism. We should never embark on a war without a very clear sense of the costs and risks, and we should never dismiss the possibility of failure. We do not normally assume that our actions will inevitably turn a suboptimal situation into something far better. Sometimes our actions make things worse.

The experiences of the past nearly two decades, including the responses to the terrorist attacks of September 11, 2001, have reaffirmed these truths and have taught all of us—not just libertarians—some important lessons. We have learned that the costs of waging wars, while they may be manageable, are rarely offset by the benefits that we derive from them. This does not mean that military intervention is never warranted. It does mean that we should clearly define those instances in which war *is* the last best course of action and that we should otherwise seek to expand the domain of liberty by peaceful means.

Part I

A Brief History of U.S. Foreign Policy

②

The American Founders, the State, and War

Classical liberals strive to limit the state's power lest it undermine the rights of the people that it is empowered to protect. And traditionally, classical liberals have been among the most passionate and consistent opponents of war, because warfare has been the principal driver of the growth of the state over the course of human history.

The liberals who carved the United States of America out of the mighty British Empire understood this well. One might say it defined their approach to governance. James Madison, as noted in chapter 1, saw war as like fertilizer for a noxious weed. "Of all enemies of public liberty," he wrote in 1795, "war is, perhaps, the most to be dreaded, because it comprises and develops the germ of every other."[1] The Founders were also skeptical of war's capacity for effecting good ends. "There never was a good war, or a bad peace," opined Benjamin Franklin.[2]

These men held these views despite the fact that they had all experienced a war that delivered to them what they most desired—a divorce from the British Crown and a chance to construct a new political order. But while this would seem to be a good end, and thus the Revolutionary War the very definition of a good war, the American patriots would have preferred to achieve their goals by peaceful means.

Skepticism of war contributed to a skepticism of the instruments for waging it. In his Farewell Address, George Washington advised his countrymen to "avoid the necessity of those overgrown military establishments which, under any form of government, are inauspicious to liberty, and which are to be regarded as particularly hostile to republican liberty."[3]

Such sentiments were widespread among the Founders, as Bruce Porter explains in his book *War and the Rise of the State*:

> The vast majority of America's landowning aristocracy had an almost congenital distrust of standing armies, which their ancestors for generations had identified with despotism. . . . They glorified instead the yeoman militiamen, linked to the land and closely tied to local interests.[4]

This faith in militiamen over professional soldiers, bordering on romanticism, occasionally crashed against the rocks of military reality. On the one hand, the Declaration of Rights adopted by the First Continental Congress on October 14, 1774, affirmed "that the keeping [of] a standing army in these colonies, in times of peace, without the consent of the legislature of that colony, in which such army is kept, is against law."[5] These sentiments were repeated in the long list of particulars included within the Declaration of Independence, which explained to all who would hear the reasons for the separation of the American colonies from the British Crown.

On the other hand, George Washington regularly bemoaned his inability to wage an effective war against British regulars with amateur soldiers. The creation of the Continental Army itself might have been seen as a betrayal of the very principles that the Founders had invoked for wanting to be free of the mother country in the first place. But the army that the colonials created was at least their own, and they were clearly in a state of war.

The U.S. Constitution strove to resolve this tension between the need for a credible national defense and the fear that a large standing army and frequent wars would upset the delicate balance between individuals and the state. The document placed strict limits on the new government's ability to go to war, and therefore also its propensity to do so, but it allowed the federal government to mobilize and deploy military power in self-defense. The Constitution granted Congress the power "to provide and maintain a Navy" but stipulated that armies would be raised and supported as needed: in other words, no standing army during peacetime. Although the idea is all but unfathomable to most Americans today, it was not so radical at the time. Most countries in that era chose to rely on a small number of professional soldiers, including mercenaries for hire, for defense or to wage war. These forces could have been augmented by private citizens but rarely were. Countries such as England, to whom the Americans looked for so many of their governing traditions, saw little need for *any* army except the relatively small cadre of regulars used to police the empire's far-flung colonies or to attempt to pry foreign lands from other European powers' clutches. The British army, in other words, was not all that important for the defense of the British Isles. The country's relatively small and quiescent population was not a mortal threat to the British government. The island itself was abundant in natural resources, and it was protected from foreign invasion by water on all sides and a quite capable navy.

The men who formed the new American government inherited their forefathers' skepticism of standing armies. They also drew lessons from antiquity. James Madison was among the most emphatic on this score. "A standing military force, with an overgrown Executive will not long be safe companions to liberty,"[6] he told his fellow delegates at the Constitutional Convention in Philadelphia. History informed his judgement:

> The means of defense against foreign danger, have been always the instruments of tyranny at home. Among the Romans it was a standing maxim to excite a war, whenever a revolt was apprehended. Throughout all Europe, the armies kept up under the pretext of defending, have enslaved the people.[7]

Madison's contemporaries echoed his warnings at the numerous state ratifying conventions. Indeed, at least some opponents of the Constitution believed that the document didn't go far enough to protect the rights of the people against the threat of standing militaries. Patrick Henry, a leader among the Anti-Federalists in Virginia, was wary, anticipating a massive imbalance between state militias and a federalized fighting force. "Will your mace-bearer be a match for a disciplined [federal] regiment?" he asked.[8] The state constitutions of Virginia and North Carolina spelled out the widespread belief that "standing armies in time[s] of peace are dangerous to liberty" and provided for the "strict subordination" of the military to civilian power.[9]

But constraining the government's ability to wage war was not enough to secure individual rights. The Founders also sought to limit the new government's propensity to declare war in the first place by granting such power to Congress rather than the executive. Madison explained the rationale in a letter to Thomas Jefferson in April 1798: "The constitution supposes, what the History of all Gov[ernmen]ts demonstrates, that the Ex[ecutive] is the branch of power most interested in war, and most prone to it. It has accordingly with studied care, vested the question of war in the [Legislature]."[10] In the Pennsylvania Ratifying Convention, the Federalist James Wilson explained that "this system will not hurry us into war; it is calculated to guard against it. It will not be in the power of a single man, or a single body of men, to involve us in such distress."[11] Madison confided his firm belief that "in no part of the constitution is more wisdom to be found, than in the clause which confides the question of war or peace to the legislature, and not to the executive department."[12]

Alexander Hamilton may not have agreed with that sentiment, but he didn't dispute that the Constitution vested the war powers with the Congress, not the executive. The legislature alone, he explained, possessed the power to initiate wars, whereas the president's powers were confined to "the direction of war when authorized or begun."[13] Anti-Federalists were skeptical of these assurances. They claimed that Hamilton and other advocates for the new Constitution were attempting to give the office of the presidency powers commensurate with the hated monarchs that the American revolutionaries had fought against. They were half right. Hamilton was generally a strong advocate for executive authority, and he supported measures that expanded the president's powers, both during the drafting and ratification of the Constitution and later as one of the leaders of President Washington's cabinet. But Hamilton forcefully rejected the Anti-Federalists' claim that he was investing the presidency with the powers of a king. Writing as Publius in *Federalist* 69, he explained, with emphasis:

> The President is to be the commander-in-chief of the army and navy of the United States. In this respect his authority would be nominally the same with that of the king of Great Britain, but in substance much inferior to it. It would amount to nothing more than the supreme command and direction of the military and naval forces, as first General and admiral of the Confederacy; while that of the British king extends to the *declaring* of war and to the *raising* and *regulating* of fleets and armies—all which, by the Constitution under consideration, would appertain to the legislature.[14]

Several years later, Hamilton and Madison disagreed about Washington's declaration of impartiality in the war between England and France. Madison sought to thwart even the hint of an executive's usurpation of the war power. "The power to declare war, including the power of judging of the causes of war," Madison forcefully reminded his interlocutor, "is *fully* and *exclusively* vested in the legislature." He went on, "The executive has no right, in any case, to decide this question, whether there is or is not cause for declaring war."[15] The president's sole role was to call Congress into session and inform it of the circumstances so that the legislature—not the president—could make a decision on the wisdom or imprudence of war.

Such notions undoubtedly strike many modern readers as unnecessarily, or even dangerously, unwieldy, and there may have been some people in the late 18th century who shared such sentiments. But the new nation's relative reluctance to become embroiled in Europe's bitter disputes reflected both the classical liberals' skepticism of war in general and the modern realists' assessment that involvement in those wars at that particular juncture would have been strategically unwise. For the most part, the first few presidents of the American republic managed to steer clear of Europe's fights.

They were able to do so largely because they followed another key piece of advice from Washington's Farewell Address: "The great rule of conduct for us, in regard to foreign nations, is in extending our commercial relations to have with them as little political connection as possible." As the nation's power grew—as Washington was sure that it would—potential belligerents would be more inclined to respect that neutrality. When that time came, Washington predicted, "we may choose peace or war, as our interest, guided by justice, shall counsel." In the meantime, however, the new nation should "steer clear of permanent alliances." It should undertake efforts to establish "a respectable defensive posture" and "safely trust to temporary alliances for extraordinary emergencies."[16]

Thomas Jefferson, though he fought bitterly with Washington as a member of his cabinet, affirmed this wisdom. The nation's first secretary of state pledged in his first inaugural address as president to pursue a foreign and military policy of "peace, commerce, and honest friendship with all nations, entangling alliances with none."[17]

Despite its relative military weakness, the young nation had the luxury of choice. "Separated as we are by a world of water from other Nations," Washington explained in a letter to a friend, "if we are wise we shall surely avoid being drawn into the labyrinth of their politics, and involved in their destructive wars." For much of the first 130 years or so of U.S. history, Americans rather successfully stayed out of foreign wars. They had little need for a standing military, especially a standing army, and what they did retain during peacetime was always quite small. On particular occasions when the Congress saw fit to declare war, for example against England in 1812 or Mexico in 1846, it also made provisions for raising the army, as stipulated in the Constitution, and providing the army with necessary materials. It was not simply ideology and adherence to principle that allowed Americans to remain true to the letter and spirit of the Constitution's limits on war and standing armies. The new nation was also blessed, as Washington had noted, by geography; powerful enemies were few, and generally far away. The foreign powers that might have occasionally aspired to take a bite out of the upstart republic always seemed more interested in other places or were more distracted by dangers closer to home.

U.S. leaders also secured some tangible benefits through wise diplomacy and good fortune. From the time of Washington's first inaugural address in 1789 to the early 1820s, the European powers' reach and influence in North America slowly but inexorably receded. Jefferson bought off the French with the Louisiana Purchase, an acquisition made possible partly by the defeat of a French garrison in Haiti; Napoleon's nascent dreams of North American conquest largely died with France's ignominious expulsion from its former colony by a violent slave revolt. America's steady pressure on Spain secured American access to the Gulf of Mexico via New Orleans and rights for passage along the Mississippi River. Then in 1819, Spain ceded Florida to the United States under the terms of the Adams–Onís Treaty.

John Quincy Adams, James Monroe's secretary of state and the principal architect of that diplomatic achievement, publicly spelled out the ideal American approach to foreign policy in a speech on July 4, 1821. He attempted to connect the ideas of the Declaration of Independence to the foreign policy of the nation that had announced itself to the world 45 years earlier:

> In the progress of forty years since the acknowledgment of our Independence, we have gone through many modifications of internal government, and through all the vicissitudes of peace and war, with other mighty nations. But never, never for a moment have the great principles, consecrated by the Declaration of this day, been renounced or abandoned.[19]

What were those principles? When people from around the world asked, "What has America done for the benefit of mankind?" Adams had a ready answer.

We had with one voice, he explained, "proclaimed to mankind the inextinguishable rights of human nature, and the only lawful foundations of government." The nation had "held forth . . . the hand of honest friendship, of equal freedom, of generous reciprocity" and "uniformly spoken among them, though often to heedless and often to disdainful ears, the language of equal liberty, equal justice, and equal rights."[20]

But while Adams believed that Americans should proclaim these principles, he was equally adamant that we not fight for them. On the contrary, the United States had "without a single exception, respected the independence of other nations, while asserting and maintaining her own. She has abstained from interference in the concerns of others, even when the conflict has been for principles to which she clings, as to the last vital drop that visits the heart."[21]

Americans understood that great contests would be fought in the ensuing centuries "between inveterate power, and emerging right."[22] But they also knew that their armed involvement in distant disputes would undermine their very claim to be an exemplar of liberty and good governance.

Adams concluded with a flourish. He was, after all, entertaining an audience of listeners attending a Fourth of July celebration. Suffice it to say he spiced it up a little. By the standards of the day, it was probably pretty mild. By 21st-century standards, it's habanero hot:

> Wherever the standard of freedom and independence
> has been or shall be unfurled, there will her heart, her

benedictions and her prayers be. But she goes not abroad in   search of monsters to destroy. She is the well-wisher to the freedom and independence of all. She is the champion and vindicator only of her own. She will recommend the general cause, by the countenance of her voice, and the benignant sympathy of her example. She well knows that by once enlisting under other banners than her own, were they even the banners of foreign independence, she would involve herself, beyond the power of extrication, in all the wars of interest and intrigue, of individual avarice, envy, and ambition, which assume the colors and usurp the standard of freedom. The fundamental maxims of her policy would insensibly change from liberty to force. The frontlet upon her brows would no longer beam with the ineffable splendor of freedom and independence; but in its stead would soon be substituted an imperial diadem, flashing in false and tarnished lustre the murky radiance of dominion and power. She might become the dictatress of the world: she would be no longer the ruler of her own spirit.[23]

Less than two years later, Adams helped draft the Monroe Doctrine, which declared that "any attempt" of a European power to exert influence in the Western Hemisphere was "dangerous to [American] peace and safety."[24] It therefore warned Europeans not to interfere in the affairs of any independent nations of the hemisphere. In return, the U.S. president pledged that the United States would remain neutral in disputes between the European states, continuing a policy pursued by his predecessors.

The Monroe Doctrine's pledge to remain aloof from foreign disputes was limited by the still-young republic's meager capacity for projecting power and influence abroad. Similarly, Monroe's bold stand for European noninterference in the Americas was built on rhetoric, not hard power. The United States lacked the authority to defend the independence of any other state in the hemisphere and likewise lacked the military power to block any such bid by force.

Monroe's threat to oppose further European colonization in the United States' backyard was never seriously tested. Exhausted by the Napoleonic Wars and fearful of domestic disturbances that might upset the delicate social and political order at home, Europe generally left the Americas alone. The Europeans turned their eyes instead toward conquest in Asia and Africa, where the indigenous populations were even less able to defend themselves than the newly independent states in North and South America.

The United States took advantage of its good fortune, generally following the model articulated by Washington and Jefferson and then reiterated by John Quincy Adams. Americans focused their attention on building the institutions of government at home and developing the nation's vast resources. They occasionally deployed military force to extend and consolidate their hold on the lands west of the Mississippi, at the expense of the various Native American tribes that resisted. But they were extremely reluctant to become embroiled in foreign conflicts. And when some Americans were tempted to move too far, or too fast, they encountered stiff resistance—as much from domestic foes as from foreign ones—as we'll explore in the next chapter.

3

The Anti-Imperial Empire

Many in America's founding generation believed that the United States would eventually achieve greatness. How it would go about doing so was often in question.

The Founders expected to do great things in the New World. A few even believed that God willed it. Though they arrived in what would come to be known as North America, some saw the territory as a New Israel, God's new chosen land.

They took their cue from the New Testament and their words from Jesus's Sermon on the Mount: "You are the light of the world. A city on a hill cannot be hidden." The Puritan leader John Winthrop invoked the phrase "city on a hill" in an address to his congregation sometime in 1630 while en route from Southampton, England, to New England in North America. Over the ensuing few centuries—but mostly in just the last few decades—the idea has transitioned, notes Hillsdale College's Richard Gamble, "from biblical metaphor to nationalist myth."[1]

Myth or not, the idea that God had bestowed his grace on the United States and its people was widely believed. His chosen people, popular belief also went, had a special obligation to spread ideas about good governance and justice, not merely within North America but ultimately throughout the world.

But the American colonists' bitter experience under British rule tempered their enthusiasm for imitating its methods in their quest to propagate their particular worldview. Many Americans harbored doubts about the scope of any given country's power and influence, and whether and how that power could justly be wielded. After all, the skepticism about whether a distant metropole could exercise effective and legitimate political control over a great and growing population was one of the defining themes of the revolution that eventually threw off the British yoke. "Small islands not capable of protecting themselves, are the proper objects for kingdoms to take under their care," scoffed Thomas Paine in *Common Sense*,

> but there is something very absurd, in supposing a continent to be perpetually governed by an island. In no instance hath nature made the satellite larger than its primary planet, and as England and America, with respect to each other, reverses the common order of nature, it is evident they belong to different systems; England to Europe, America to itself.[2]

Many of the Founders, and their descendants, held similar views. For the few and small to dominate the many and large defied common sense. Resistance to imperialism, British style or otherwise, thus persisted well into the 20th century and beyond.

On the other hand, Paine's sense of what the Americans might achieve should they gain independence from England was breathtaking in its grandiosity. Indeed, it was biblical—this time of the

Old Testament variety. "We have it in our power to begin the world over again," he predicted. "A situation, similar to the present, hath not happened since the days of Noah until now. The birthday of a new world is at hand."[3]

In the late 18th or early 19th century, it was preposterous to think that the new nation tucked along the Atlantic seaboard in North America could wield power over others many thousands of miles away, as the British had effectively done. But as the United States prospered and grew, so did its influence.

Americans' views on the question of what type of empire the United States could be, and should be, evolved over time. In the earliest days of independence, before the ratification of the new Constitution, Thomas Jefferson labeled the United States the "Empire *of* Liberty." It would offer freedom to those already on the land and to new immigrants from the Old World. A quarter century later, after the U.S. government had enacted the Northwest Ordinance and completed the Louisiana Purchase, Jefferson envisioned the United States as a great "Empire *for* Liberty." "Jefferson's revision," explains historian Richard Immerman, "signaled a commitment to a more aggressive, proactive extension of that sphere of liberty," throughout the New World, and perhaps someday beyond it.[4]

This was more than a semantic distinction. Immerman notes that "empire" was not a loaded term in the late 18th century. Empire did not *per se* signal exploitation or necessarily imply illegitimate rule.

The American colonists who rose up against their colonial masters objected to the manner in which Britain ruled them, not its being a nascent empire. Indeed, one of the grievances against the British Crown that the revolutionaries cited as a reason for separation was the *prohibition* on westward expansion after the French and Indian Wars. In other words, they were offended that the British Empire was denying them the right to exploit neighboring territories.

After the Treaty of Paris, which formalized the former colonies' separation, the unshackled Americans got busy growing. And with each successive generation, the hunger for new land drove them inexorably west. In this sense, a number of Native American communities saw the new United States as a far more oppressive colonizer than the British Empire that came before.

Americans justified territorial expansion throughout the contiguous landmass of North America on both economic and security grounds. They also had an eye on lands separated by water: Cuba, Santo Domingo, and other Caribbean isles; then Hawaii and the Philippines; and later Panama. By the early 20th century, the United States had in fact acquired a collection of colonies through conquest and coercive diplomacy rivaling that of many traditional European empires, though not yet close to that of Great Britain at the time.

The single factor that may have differentiated the United States from other colonial empires was not the scale of its expansion, but the reluctance that accompanied it. The United States is, writes Immerman, "an imperialist with a history of opposing imperialism." It encountered "an unprecedented amount of trouble imposing its will on its dependents."[5] In the raucous rough and tumble of American politics, there were always those who accused their political adversaries of betraying the nation's most cherished principles whenever some major territorial acquisition was in the offing. Such charges were invariably answered by loud protestations to the contrary. "Americans' self-image as the bastion of liberty and their identification with the Constitution," which enshrined classical liberals' ideas about the proper balance between the government and the people it served, Immerman explains, constrained both the politics and practice of the American empire.[6]

Louisiana

American history students are taught that Thomas Jefferson's 1803 purchase of the vast territory of Louisiana from France was a signature achievement of his presidency and an essential step on the path to American greatness. Even those historians who were not generally inclined to extol Jefferson and his governing philosophy were effusive in their praise. Henry Adams recorded that the acquisition of Louisiana had been "an event so portentous as to defy measurement" and an "unparalleled" diplomatic move.[7]

The price was a bargain: 828,000 square miles at a cost of $15 million, a mere 4 cents per acre. It paved the way for westward expansion, eventually all the way to the Pacific. The acquisition of Louisiana eliminated any lingering French threat in North America and removed a buffer between the United States and Spain, bringing new pressure to bear on the declining Spanish empire. Jefferson saw the Louisiana Purchase as a key component of his vision for creating an Empire of Liberty.

But while most Americans at the time shared Jefferson's enthusiasm, some questioned the move. Many of these criticisms were grounded in classical liberals' anxieties about the dangerous growth of state power, particularly in the realm of foreign affairs. Jefferson had clearly violated the limited and enumerated powers of the Constitution in concluding the purchase without Congress's approval. By what authority, critics wondered, had he pledged to dramatically expand the supposedly limited federal government's dominion and pay this substantial sum?

Jefferson had to overcome his own qualms about the purchase. The Constitution, he noted, "made no provision for our holding foreign territory, still less for incorporating foreign nations into our Union." To Sen. John Breckinridge of Kentucky, he confided that his unilateral executive action clearly constituted "an act beyond the Constitution."[8]

On the other hand, Jefferson was worried that Bonaparte would change his mind and renege on the agreement. Jefferson therefore hoped to conclude the deal quickly and avoid needless delays. His cabinet officers, including his secretary of state, James Madison, convinced him that a constitutional amendment was unnecessary. Jefferson convened a special session of Congress in October 1803 to approve the sale and pass the necessary companion legislation. The Senate vote far exceeded the required two-thirds for treaty ratification—a mere five senators voted against—and the House swiftly passed legislation providing the necessary funds.

The dissenters, primarily anti-Jeffersonian Federalists from New England, were a minority within a minority. The few Louisiana holdouts were accused of playing politics or downright treachery. Partisanship and a visceral distrust of Jefferson clearly played a role in their opposition. But these men, including Sens. James

Hillhouse of Connecticut, Timothy Pickering of Massachusetts, and William Plumer of New Hampshire, were among the first to display a fealty for Constitutional principles that might—and they said should—supersede the drive for territorial expansion. Pickering went so far as to propose northern disunion in 1804. Pickering's plan, notes historian David Mayers, "was based upon defensible concern for the Constitution, understandable anxiety about the shifting balance of power between north and south, and premonitions of a stormy future centered on the slavery question."[9]

The Federalists' strong opposition to the expansion of slavery was multifaceted. It was partly political. The three-fifths clause of the Constitution had granted slave-owning states such as Virginia a numerical advantage in Congress and the Electoral College. The Federalists, concentrated in northern states, had seen this numbers game play to their disadvantage when Jefferson, a Virginian, bested the sitting president John Adams, from Massachusetts, in the election of 1800. The addition of more slave-holding states from the newly acquired Louisiana Territory threatened to deepen the Federalists' electoral distress.

But the Louisiana dissenters also offered a moral argument against the expansion of U.S. territory and thus the spread of what Senator Hillhouse called "a serious evil." Hillhouse also worried that the expansion of slavery into Louisiana would threaten national security. Because "these slaves [were] men [with the] the passions and feelings of men," the danger of slave rebellion was ever present.[10] Louisiana dissenters recounted horrific tales from white refugees of the slave rebellion in Saint-Domingue (modern-day Haiti) to buttress this point. The need to extinguish this danger would necessitate a standing army to keep the peace, an idea that was anathema to the Federalists—and another clear violation of the Constitution.

Such arguments failed to persuade most Americans. The right of slave-owners to carry into the new territories what the law recognized as property was never seriously in question. Slave-owners alleged that only Africans could safely cultivate the land, whereas whites would struggle to survive in the oppressive heat and humidity of the Deep South. Ensuring the most efficient use of this vast land, of importance to both the northern and southern economies, thus depended—so the argument went—upon slavery. The brief but heated debate over Louisiana presaged later arguments about slavery that would eventually tear the nation apart. They next played out in the debate over another major territorial expansion: the admission of Texas to the Union and the accession of former Mexican lands.

War with Mexico

"The United States," notes historian George Herring, "had long coveted Texas," and in the 1840s other Mexican territories, including California and modern-day New Mexico, "also became objects of desire."[11]

The rationales in favor of acquiring these lands echoed those from the brief debate over Louisiana—especially the idea that American security and prosperity both depended on territorial expansion. But the presence of over 30,000 former U.S. citizens who had accepted the Mexican government's offer of cheap cotton-growing land added a distinctive flavor to the Texas debate.

These men had uprooted their families—and their slaves—and moved west, but they soon grew tired of what they perceived to be an overly intrusive Mexican government meddling in their business affairs. Concern that Mexico might ban the use of slave labor only heightened the recent arrivals' anxiety. When they declared Texas an independent state in 1836, the Mexican government attempted to put down the revolt. It instead got a war with the United States that would ultimately result in a humiliating defeat and the loss of 40 percent of its territory.

The Texas rebels had successfully drawn the U.S. government to their side. In truth, it didn't take that much effort; President James K. Polk, an avowed expansionist, was only too happy for the opportunity.

But not all Americans were as enthused as Polk about Texas's accession to the Union, specifically, or territorial expansion generally.

Some questioned the wisdom or even the need to expand for the purposes of defending the United States from foreign threats. The likelihood of such threats materializing, they said, was vanishingly small. According to a 28-year-old Abraham Lincoln in a speech in his hometown of Springfield, Illinois, the greater danger came from within:

> At what point shall we expect the approach of danger? By what means shall we fortify against it? Shall we expect some transatlantic military giant, to step the Ocean, and crush us at a blow? Never! All the armies of Europe, Asia and Africa combined, with all the treasure of the earth (our own excepted) in their military chest; with a

Buonaparte for a commander, could not by force, take a drink from the Ohio, or make a track on the Blue Ridge, in a trial of a thousand years.

At what point then is the approach of danger to be expected? I answer, if it ever reach us, it must spring up amongst us. It cannot come from abroad. If destruction be our lot, we must ourselves be its author and finisher. As a nation of freemen, we must live through all time, or die by suicide.[12]

Others voiced similar concerns. Daniel Webster fretted over the "dangerous tendency and doubtful consequences to enlarge the boundaries of this country, or the territories over which our laws are now established." "If we would make our institutions permanent," Webster continued, "there must be some limit to the extent of our territory."[13]

Several years later, Webster opposed the Mexican War on the same grounds: expanding the United States far beyond its current borders would weaken the institutions of government. He said:

We want no extension of territory, we want no accession of new States. The country is already large enough. I do not speak of any cession which may be made in the establishment of boundaries, or of the acquisition of a port or two on the Pacific, for the benefit of navigation and commerce. But I speak of large territories, obtained by conquest, to form States to be annexed to the Union; and I say I am opposed to such acquisition altogether.[14]

Webster and other northerners correctly worried that the new states acquired from the Mexican War would likely be slave states, upsetting the delicate balance of power in Congress that had been established in the Missouri Compromise of 1820. But they also complained of how the Mexican War had provided an opening for President Polk to circumvent some of the most cherished principles of the Constitution, including especially Congress's control over the war power.

In 1846, Polk had sent American troops into territory claimed jointly by Mexico and the United States. When Mexican forces attacked U.S. General Zachary Taylor's contingent, Congress declared war. Polk had effectively circumvented Congress in order to precipitate a conflict. Two years later, Congress formally censured Polk for exceeding his authority, but by then the damage had already been done: Polk's actions had disturbed the peace and upset the balance between the executive and Congress.

Polk's actions caught the attention—and ire—of a young lawmaker from Illinois. "Allow the President to invade a neighboring nation, whenever he shall deem it necessary to repel an invasion," wrote Abraham Lincoln in a letter to his law partner, "and you allow him to do so, whenever he may choose to say he deems it necessary for such purposes—and you allow him to make war at pleasure." He went on:

> The provision of the Constitution giving the war making power to Congress, was dictated, as I understand it, by the following reasons. Kings had always been involving and impoverishing their people in wars, pretending

generally, if not always, that the good of the people was the object. This, our convention understood to be the most oppressive of all kingly oppressions; and they resolved to so frame the Constitution that no one man should hold the power of bringing this oppression upon us.[15]

Lincoln understood this history, but Polk understood power. He wouldn't be the last president to exceed his authority in the quest to expand the boundaries of the United States. He also wouldn't be the last president forced to contend with the opponents of such expansion. The most consequential period of territorial expansion concerned the acquisition of faraway lands, chiefly islands separated by hundreds or many thousands of miles of water from the American people and the American government. The next chapter focuses on the spirited debate occasioned by the United States' brief war with Spain and especially by its handling of Spain's former colony, the Philippines.

$$\bigodot 4$$

Imperialists Triumphant?

The hardcore anti-imperialists tried and failed to block the extension of America's dominion over the entirety of the temperate latitudes in North America between the Atlantic and Pacific Oceans. Each successive wave of territorial expansion invoked a similar set of justifications, and all could be traced to a reasonable attempt to establish a security perimeter within which the peoples of the United States could prosper and grow in peace. Americans desired ample arable land. They obtained it. They needed navigable waterways. They developed those. They needed a buffer against potential adversaries. They established that.

By the late 19th century, however, it became harder to justify territorial expansion on those same terms. When Secretary of State William Seward negotiated a deal to purchase Alaska from Russia in 1867, his critics lampooned it as "Seward's Icebox." Congress ultimately appropriated the $7.2 million, but several years later, the Senate rejected President Ulysses S. Grant's treaty to annex Santo Domingo.

A new dynamic was driving the quest for new territories in far-flung places. The need for coaling stations to fuel a growing fleet of commercial steamships, and then the U.S. Navy ships to protect them, served as the justification for the acquisition of not merely islands in the nearby Caribbean, but also far more distant outposts in the vast Pacific Ocean. The key to national greatness, explained U.S. Navy Captain Alfred Thayer Mahan, was control of the seas, made possible by a strong and active navy. This approach explicitly rejected the policy recommended by America's founders and followed for over a century. "I am frankly an imperialist," Mahan wrote, "in the sense that no nation, certainly no great nation, should henceforth maintain the policy of isolation which fitted our early history. . . . Imperialism, the extension of national authority over alien communities, is a dominant note in the world politics of today."[1]

Others were motivated by humanitarian considerations. Even some skeptics of overseas territorial expansion by conquest justified it—or at least tolerated it—on the grounds that war with Spain in 1898 would liberate people struggling against foreign oppression. Newspapers peddled sensational stories about a revolution in nearby Cuba, always portraying Spain as the villain. The February 1898 destruction under dubious circumstances of the battleship USS *Maine* in Havana Harbor stoked war fever (jingoes naturally blamed Spain): "Remember the *Maine*, to hell with Spain." From there, it was a relatively small step to the country's first major war with a European country in over 75 years.

Expansionists used the war to secure America's status as a world power. President William McKinley asserted that "we must keep all we get" until the war ended. And once "the war is over we must keep what we want."[2] These new acquisitions eventually included Puerto Rico in the Caribbean and Guam and Wake Atoll in the Pacific.

The most important prize, however, was arguably Hawaii, and that wasn't even a Spanish possession. The island chain had been governed since 1893 by mostly American planters and missionaries who had deposed the island's monarchy. They appealed to U.S. leaders, first Grover Cleveland and later McKinley, to formally annex the islands lest they fall into the hands of less-friendly powers such as Japan. But Cleveland firmly declined, and McKinley initially exhibited little enthusiasm for the endeavor.

After the start of the Spanish–American War, however—with Hawaii serving as a crucial way station for U.S. troops on their way to the Philippines—McKinley concluded, "We need Hawaii just as much and a good deal more than we did California. It is manifest destiny."[3]

The prospect alarmed some Americans. Sen. Stephen White of California summed up anti-imperialist anxieties. "If we consummate this scheme" to take possession of Hawaii, he predicted, "we will be told we must have the Philippines, because Hawaii is not worth much unless we can have something else to use it for. And when we have annexed the Philippines we must have something else. So we will extend our action around the globe and enter upon an imperialistic policy."[4]

White's warning proved prophetic. The acquisition of the Philippines following the end of the brief Spanish–American War proved a step too far for a number of other Americans. If the U.S. government could justify expanding its writ to an archipelago of islands more than 8,500 miles away from Washington,

DC, then there was no practical limit to what it could do or what the United States might ultimately entail. A loose coalition of anti-imperialists rose in opposition and took their case to the American people.

The leading arguments against overseas expansion echoed John Quincy Adams's warnings from 1821. For example, anti-imperialists meeting at Boston's Faneuil Hall on June 15, 1898, adopted by acclamation a resolution affirming, in part, that:

> The mission of the United States is to help the world by an example of successful self-government, and that to abandon the principles and the policy under which we have prospered, and embrace the doctrine and practices now called imperial, is to enter the path which, with other great republics, has ended in the downfall of free institutions. . . . [Our] first duty is to cure the evils of our own country.[5]

Preserving America's liberal institutions and norms proved a particularly important message for the national Anti-Imperialist League. Its platform, adopted in October 1899, declared:

> Much as we abhor the war of "criminal aggression" in the Philippines, greatly as we regret that the blood of the Filipinos is on American hands, we more deeply resent the betrayal of American institutions at home. The real firing line is not in the suburbs of Manila. The foe is of our own household. The attempt of 1861 was to divide the country. That of 1899 is to destroy its fundamental principles.[6]

The league drew support from literary figures such as Mark Twain, William Dean Howells, and Ambrose Bierce; college presidents and prominent academics; at least two former presidents (Grover Cleveland and Benjamin Harrison); and the leading Democrat of the day, William Jennings Bryan. Industrialist Andrew Carnegie found common cause with labor leader Samuel Gompers. Reformist thinkers and writers such as *The Nation* editor E. L. Godkin joined forces with social activists like Jane Addams.

Many other leading anti-imperialists were refugees from the Republican Party. Derisively called "mugwumps," they were often dismissed as sanctimonious dreamers with little interest in the practical business of governing.[7] But some mainstream Republicans also resisted overseas expansion. As noted, former president Benjamin Harrison raised objections to the war, as did former treasury secretary George Boutwell and McKinley's own secretary of state, John Sherman. Thomas Brackett Reed from Maine, the Republican Speaker of the House from 1889 to 1891 and again from 1895 to 1899, opposed the Spanish–American war, the annexation of Hawaii, and the campaign to subdue the recalcitrant Filipinos.[8]

McKinley had concluded that the entirety of the Philippine archipelago—7,000 islands totaling over 115,000 square miles populated by seven million people of diverse ethnicity—must be brought under the control of the United States.[9] He was motivated by more than geopolitics. He felt responsibility for bringing stability to the islands while minimizing bloodshed during the transition away from Spanish rule. He also believed that Americans had a humanitarian obligation to the Filipinos. "There was nothing left for us to do but to take them all," he told a group of visitors to the White House, "and educate . . . and uplift and Christianize them, and by God's grace do the very best we could by them, as our fellow-men for whom Christ also died."[10]

It would be a mistake to dismiss this as "hypocritical hogwash," writes historian Walter McDougall. "In fact, religious sentiment was instrumental in rallying the American people . . . to an imperial mission."[11]

The cleverest of the imperialists, however, combined a divine mission with claims of racial superiority while invoking American greatness. For example, after returning from a trip to the Philippines in December 1899, Indiana's Albert Beveridge exulted in a Senate-floor speech, "Thanksgiving to Almighty God that He has marked us as His chosen people."[12] To turn away from this calling, to refuse to take up what the British writer Rudyard Kipling had called the "white man's burden," would betray not merely American ideals, but the hopes and dreams of countless generations.

"God has not been preparing the English-speaking and Teutonic peoples for a thousand years for nothing but vain and idle self-contemplation and self-admiration," Beveridge thundered. "No! He has made us the master organizers of the world to establish system where chaos reigns. . . . Were it not for such a force as this the world would relapse into barbarism and night. . . . We are trustees of the world's progress, guardians of its righteous peace."[13]

Others were unconvinced, however. George Boutwell, the first president of the Anti-Imperialist League, was a prominent abolitionist as well as an accomplished politician. He reasoned, explains author Stephen Kinzer, that "every abolitionist was a natural anti-imperialist, since anyone who opposed keeping human beings as slaves must also oppose ruling other peoples against their will."[14]

Similarly, George Frisbie Hoar of Massachusetts, one of only two Senate Republicans to vote against the treaty with Spain, rejected the very notion that land and peoples could be bought and sold "or won as spoils of war or prizes in battle." Such a doctrine may have been deemed suitable "in the ancient and barbarous laws of war. But it has no place under the American Constitution. It has no place where the Declaration of Independence is a living reality."[15]

Hoar complained to his Senate colleagues that acquisition of Spain's former colonies was inconsistent with the American principles set forth at the nation's founding and consecrated in blood during the American Civil War. Abraham Lincoln had said, "No man was ever created good enough to own another." Likewise, Hoar concluded, "No nation was ever created good enough to own another."[16]

Some anti-imperialists, including many southern Democrats, viewed the Filipinos as hopelessly backward and lacking the intellect and temperament for self-government. They imagined a host of horrors that might befall the republic if these distant islanders were ever granted rights as citizens. Champ Clark, a representative from Missouri, disdained the notion that "almond eyed, brown skinned United States Senators" might someday serve beside him in Congress. "No matter whether they are fit to govern themselves or not, they are not fit to govern us."[17] The odious Senator "Pitchfork Ben" Tillman, a white supremacist from

South Carolina, objected to introducing into the "body politic of the United States . . . that vitiated blood, that debase and ignorant people."[18]

Pro-expansion Republicans often turned the tables on anti-imperialists by observing that their concerns about human rights and principles of equality were purely situational. Theodore Roosevelt remarked acidly to Harvard president Charles William Eliot about southern Democrats:

> [They] prate about the doctrines contained in the Declaration of Independence, as applied to brown men in the Philippines, [even as] they themselves owe their . . . influence in the nation, solely to the fact that they embody a living negation of those doctrines so far as they concern the black man at home.[19]

Roosevelt had a point. Then again, the imperialists were rarely great defenders of racial justice. Many justified expansion on explicitly racial grounds, and few held the liberated peoples in particularly high regard. The Cubans, explained General William Shafter, who had commanded U.S. forces on the island, were no more fit for self-government than "gunpowder is for hell."[20] Jacob Schurman, who headed McKinley's Philippine Commission, described the Filipinos as "amazingly credulous with childish grasp of actual facts." Instead, they possessed "great cunning, unbounded suspicion, [and] primitive passions [that were] uncontrollable when once aroused."[21]

Roosevelt himself said, among other things, that humankind's rise from barbarism to civility could mostly be attributed to "expansion of the peoples of white, or European, blood." [22] Crushing the Filipino insurrection became a conflict of "civilization," in Roosevelt's words, against the "black chaos of savagery and barbarism."[23]

When the imperialists stressed the benevolence of their mission, they encountered a different type of resistance. William Howard Taft, whom McKinley appointed as the first civil governor of the Philippines, stated that his aim was to enable his "little brown brothers" to eventually take care of themselves.[24] The Americans, he explained, would focus on building transportation and communication infrastructure while improving health and building a rule of law.

Some Americans, especially racial minorities and the poor, pointed out that such grand endeavors in faraway places were competing with similar projects closer to home. Might some of the aid bestowed on Filipinos, they asked, be put to similar use to help Americans?

"If the moral sense of the American people would not leave the distant Filipino his pitiable fate, but impelled them to reach out a saving hand across the sea and snatch him within the ennobling circle of benevolent assimilation," Professor Kelly Miller of Howard University wondered aloud, "how much more incumbent is it to elevate the Negro who is within our gates?" Edward Cooper, editor of the *Colored American*, observed dryly, "Our white friends have a habit of expending their sympathy upon the black man who is farthest off."[25]

Booker T. Washington, the most famous African American of his day, sounded a similar note of caution during a rally in Chicago convened to celebrate the American victory over Spain and attended by President McKinley. The United States, Washington allowed, "has been most fortunate in her victories," but Americans still had to "conquer ourselves in the blotting out of racial prejudices."

Failure to secure this final victory, he warned, "shall [leave], especially in the southern part of our country, a cancer gnawing at the heart of this Republic that shall one day prove as dangerous as an attack from an army from without or within."[26]

Others among the anti-imperialists noted that good intentions were being undone by violence. Charles Francis Adams confessed "I turn green in bed at midnight if I think of the horror of a year's warfare in the Philippines [where] we must slaughter a million or two of foolish Malays in order to give them the comforts of flannel petticoats and electric railways."[27]

Unsurprisingly, many Filipino nationalists were unimpressed by the Americans' exertions on their behalf. Manuel Quezon, who served alongside insurgent leader Emilio Aguinaldo and would later go on to become president of the Philippines, declared, "I would prefer a government run like hell by Filipinos to one run like heaven by Americans."[28]

The social scientist William Graham Sumner captured the anti-imperialists' rage in a celebrated speech at Yale University on January 16, 1899. Provocatively titled "The Conquest of the United States by Spain," Sumner contended that Spain was the very epitome of an imperialistic state and that the United States had been since its founding "the chief representative of the revolt and reaction against that kind of a state." Expansion and imperialism, Sumner continued, would entail "throwing away some of the most important elements of the American symbol" and adopting those of Spain.[29]

Sumner foresaw resistance to American rule not so different from that which brought down the Spanish Empire. The fatal flaw in the imperialist vision was its inability to accommodate the subject people's desire to be left alone. Americans especially, Sumner inveighed, must understand the importance of self-determination. "The doctrine that all men are equal has come to stand as one of the corner-stones of the temple of justice and truth. It was set up as a bar to just this notion that we are so much better than others that it is liberty for them to be governed by us."

Sumner also anticipated that the decision to "take away from other nations any possessions of theirs which we think we could manage better than they are managing them," and the notion that the United States should "take in hand any countries which we do not think capable of self-government," would take America in a very dangerous direction.

"War, debt, taxation, diplomacy, a grand governmental system, pomp, glory, a big army and navy, lavish expenditures, political jobbery—in a word, imperialism," would, he predicted, "hasten the day when our present advantages will wear out," and the United States would become no different than the "older and densely populated nations" of the world.

Sumner saw in the imperialists' enthusiasm for expansion abroad a tendency toward grandiose promises and foolishly ambitious objectives, all at a time when the nation was struggling to deal with problems ranging from vicious racism to rampant political corruption. The imperialists say "that Americans can do anything. They say that they do not shrink from responsibilities. They are willing to run into a hole, trusting to luck and cleverness to get out."

He continued:

> Upon a little serious examination the off-hand disposal of an important question of policy by the declaration that Americans can do anything proves to be only a silly piece of bombast, and upon a little reflection we find our hands are quite full at home of problems by the solution of which the peace and happiness of the American people could be greatly increased.

The United States was not immune to error. There were real limits to what it could do in the world, and to admit as much was not unpatriotic. On the contrary, those who waved away America's limited power and claimed that it could do anything ignored why the Founders imposed such restrictions in the first place: to preserve a republic and prevent the rise of monarchy. "We cannot govern dependencies consistently with our political system," Sumner concluded, "and . . . if we try it, the State which our fathers founded will suffer a reaction which will transform it into another empire just after the fashion of all the old ones."[30]

George Frisbie Hoar picked up on this theme a month later during debate over ratification of the Treaty of Paris that formally ended war with Spain. He warned that efforts to stifle self-rule in America's colonies would undercut liberalism at home:

> If a strong people try to govern a weak one against its will, the home government will get despotic too. You cannot

maintain despotism in Asia and a republic in America. If you try to deprive even a savage or a barbarian of his just rights you can never do it without becoming a savage or a barbarian yourself.[31]

McKinley scoffed at such arguments. On February 16, 1899, in a major speech in Boston—one of the epicenters of anti-imperialist sentiment—McKinley declared that the United States had acted on behalf of "the welfare and happiness and the rights of the inhabitants of the Philippine Islands."

He briefly conceded that "the people there had not given their consent," but he concluded that "it is not a good time for the liberator to submit important questions concerning liberty and government to the liberated while they are engaged in shooting down their rescuers."[32]

McKinley and other imperialists might have dwelled a bit longer on why the liberated were shooting in the first place. "Part of the problem," explains McKinley biographer Robert Merry, "was a misconception of Philippine society and the inhabitants' view of the U.S. arrival. The idea, shared by most Washington officials, including McKinley, was that Aguinaldo represented a small minority of Tagalog people and that most other Filipinos would embrace the U.S. presence as soon as they perceived McKinley's promised benevolence. Then they would assist in bringing down the insurgency."[33]

When that didn't occur, McKinley called on the U.S. Army to put it down. He also appointed colonial governors who reported directly to him, further expanding the power of the executive branch.

The war to suppress the Filipino insurgency damaged liberalism at home in other ways. When U.S. troops were engaged in pitched battles on foreign soil, opponents and dissenters were accused of siding with America's enemies—in other words, treason.

Henry Cabot Lodge, a leader of the imperialist faction in the Senate, implicated the opponents of the counterinsurgency campaign in the killing of American soldiers. "I vote with the army that wears the uniform and carries the flag of my country," he said. Americans were entitled to raise questions only after "the enemy has yielded and the war is over."[34]

General Frederick Funston, who achieved national renown for capturing insurgent leader Aguinaldo, boasted that he had "personally strung up thirty-five Filipinos without trial." He suggested that Americans who questioned the war deserved a similar fate. Dissenters at home, he declared, should "be dragged out of their homes and lynched."[35]

Even Nelson Miles, the army's commanding general, ran afoul of the imperialists' ire. Miles, who had earned the Congressional Medal of Honor during the Civil War and then gained further fame during the wars along the western frontier, balked when Americans turned their attention to putting down the rebellion in the Philippines. He worried that army discipline would break down as U.S. troops struggled against elusive insurgents, and he privately warned President Theodore Roosevelt that the alleged crimes already committed in the Philippines were far worse than anything the U.S. Army had inflicted on the Native Americans in North America. When Miles went public with his concerns, Roosevelt branded him a "traitor," and privately lambasted him as "the most insidious enemy which the army has had during my term of public life."[36]

In short, though McKinley and others derided the suggestion that the acquisition of vast overseas territories might cause the United States to abandon its constitutional principles, the anti-imperialists could justifiably claim that this is precisely what happened. The United States turned its back on self-government, a cornerstone of its founding texts. The power of the central government grew in order to prosecute the Spanish–American War. And the war and its aftermath undermined liberalism and free expression at home.

* * *

"No war ever transformed us quite as the war with Spain transformed us," wrote an approving Woodrow Wilson, then president of Princeton University, in 1902. "The nation has stepped forth into the open arena of the world."[37] Wilson exulted in Americans' renewed sense of purpose and was pleased with how the war had healed sectional divisions that had been torn open by the Civil War.

Others, however, mourned America's transformation. George Frisbie Hoar lamented:

> We crushed the only republic in Asia. We made war against the only Christian people in the East. We converted a war of glory to a war of shame. We vulgarized the American flag. We introduced perfidy into the practice of

war. We inflicted torture on unarmed men to extort confession. We put children to death. We established reconcentrado camps. We devastated provinces. We baffled the aspirations of a people for liberty.[38]

"The United States went off the rails," concludes historian Walter McDougall, with emphasis, "when it *went to war with Spain in the first place*. . . . It was precisely the sort of temptation that Washington and Hamilton scorned, Jefferson and Madison felt but resisted, and John Quincy Adams damned with eloquence. Exceptionalism [for them] meant liberty at home, not crusades to change the world."[39]

But that had all changed by 1898. Most Americans were amenable to embarking on the expansionists' "bold new venture," notes Robert Merry, "so long as it was executed smoothly and at an acceptable cost."[40]

Nevertheless, anti-imperial sentiment still lingered below the surface. David Mayers summarizes America's adventure into overseas empire as follows: First, it was "piddling" compared to the practice of others. Second, Americans were not willing to fight other great powers over these new possessions; the potential benefits simply didn't warrant taking great risks to secure them. Indeed, even Theodore Roosevelt had concluded by 1907 that the Philippines might become a geopolitical liability. Lastly, notes Mayers, "Americans were tentative, in some sense abashed by their imperium and nervous about the cost of colonial upkeep." Accordingly, he concludes, "an informal empire abroad was better suited to American tastes."[41]

America's spectacular rise to power and prominence through the late 19th century and into the 20th century was always tempered by the classical liberals' concerns about limiting the power of the state and avoiding unnecessary wars. The next chapter explores the further evolution of U.S. foreign policy from its small-government roots to a more expansive vision of liberalism—one that largely discarded concerns about the growing power of the state and saw U.S. military power as critical for advancing individual liberty and human rights.

$$\widehat{5}$$

The World Wars and Their Lessons

The military interventions of the late 19th and early 20th centuries whetted American leaders' appetites for playing a more active international role but did not suffice to alter the United States' fundamental approach to the rest of the world. The experience of World Wars I and II—and the lessons drawn from them—did. This chapter explores this evolution from half-hearted imperialism to full-throated global dominance.

* * *

On the surface, the Spanish–American War was a decisive victory for the expansionists. America's leaders had ignored the anti-imperialists' warnings, launched a war against Spain, and taken possession of the dying empire's former colonies, including nearby Puerto Rico and the far-off Philippines. The acquisition of significant foreign territories, and the need to administer them, provided the impetus for accelerating the expansion of an already-growing U.S. Navy. Some of these new territories provided convenient coaling stations for the growing U.S. fleet. The U.S. Army also grew, from 25,000 before the war to 100,000 after.[1]

Anxiety persisted, however, over the United States' becoming a colonial power in its own right. And there were limits to how far U.S. presidents would go. Even Theodore Roosevelt, a leading advocate for territorial expansion, occasionally resisted the temptation to use the U.S. military's rising power merely because he could. Regarding expansion into Hispaniola, Roosevelt quipped, "I have about the same desire to annex it [the Dominican Republic] as a gorged boa constrictor might have to swallow a porcupine wrong-end-to."[2]

History and logic teach that as states grow wealthier and more powerful, they seek additional ways to shape their security environment. They push the boundaries of what they consider to be their vital areas and interests, often to encompass not merely the people and territories under their formal control, but also as a buffer between themselves and others. Within these spheres of influence, the dominant power exercises de facto control and prevents the other states in this sphere from making common cause with a potential challenger. A weak and divided United States in the early 19th century might have claimed a security zone throughout Central and South America, but it was in no position to enforce it. As noted earlier, the Monroe Doctrine largely held because the European powers were too divided and because Great Britain's interests in the Western Hemisphere generally aligned with those of the United States.

But by the early 20th century, the United States had grown to become the dominant player in the Western Hemisphere through a combination of diplomacy and economic pressure, backed up at times by the use of force. Leaders in Washington, having displaced Spain from the Western Hemisphere, were determined to prevent other European powers from securing a beachhead in America's strategic backyard. The Platt Amendment, for example, blocked Cuba from making treaties granting other countries control over its foreign affairs, and accorded special rights to the United States. The Roosevelt Corollary to the Monroe Doctrine operated as a de facto Platt Amendment to all of the states in the Western Hemisphere, keeping European interests at bay while enabling the United States to intervene militarily to restore political order, or merely as its whims dictated. Wherever U.S. officials detected "chronic wrongdoing, or an impotence which results in the general loosening of the ties of civil society," Roosevelt explained, the United States was entitled to employ "an international police power" to set the natives straight.[3]

A succession of U.S. presidents intervened in the region under the aegis of the Roosevelt Corollary, starting with Roosevelt himself, who sent U.S. forces back to Cuba in 1906. William Howard Taft dispatched troops to Honduras in 1911 and Nicaragua in 1912. Woodrow Wilson sent hundreds of U.S. Marines to occupy Haiti in July 1915; they remained there until 1934. He dispatched U.S. troops into Mexico in early 1916 on a punitive expedition to hunt down Francisco "Pancho" Villa. That same year, Wilson also dispatched the U.S. military to the Dominican Republic.

Although many scholars look back on this period as one of the darker episodes in American history (a de facto bad-neighbor foreign policy), such behavior is broadly consistent with traditional approaches to security. The United States was establishing a sphere of influence in the Western Hemisphere, warning possible interlopers away.

But U.S. leaders began to expand the definition of what was required in order to be safe. It wasn't enough to keep rapacious European powers out of America's backyard. The United States pledged to maintain an Open Door to trade with Asian countries (and would try to prevent European countries from closing it).

U.S. leaders also began to take an interest in other states' internal affairs. Woodrow Wilson was willing to use force to teach Latin Americans how to "elect good men" as leaders. In April 1914, several years before the Pancho Villa expedition, Wilson dispatched U.S. troops to oust the Mexican dictator Victoriano Huerta.[4]

Wilson returned to this theme of democracy promotion when he prevailed upon his fellow Americans to enter the war in Europe in the spring of 1917. When he went before the Congress requesting a declaration of war against Germany, Wilson explained: "The world must be made safe for democracy. Its peace must be planted upon the tested foundations of political liberty." As for America's motivations, Wilson said, they were pure and benign: "We have no selfish ends to serve. We desire no conquest, no dominion. We seek no indemnities for ourselves, no material compensation for the sacrifices we shall freely make. We are but one of the champions of the rights of mankind. We shall be satisfied when those rights have been made as secure as the faith and the freedom of nations can make them."[5]

Wilson may not have desired material compensation or indemnities from others. By committing U.S. troops to the continent before the war ended, however, Wilson purchased a place at the big kids' table. He was determined that the United States never give it up thereafter.

But not every American was so willing to abandon George Washington's great rule against permanent alliances or John Quincy Adams's admonition that the United States ought to be the champion for freedom everywhere but the armed vindicator only of her own. Such notions had informed U.S. foreign policy for most of the 19th century. The heated debate over ratification of the Versailles Treaty, which would have included the United States in the League of Nations, reflected the last gasps of the noninterventionist tradition in American history.

The opposition to U.S. membership in the league—led by Woodrow Wilson's nemesis, Henry Cabot Lodge—objected that presidents could use the league to circumvent Congress's power to declare war. Collective security treaties, the opponents explained, might draw the United States into a foreign conflagration without a congressional debate, let alone a national debate.

Such warnings seemed prophetic in the wake of the second world war. Franklin Roosevelt secured near-unanimous congressional support for a declaration of war against Japan following the attack on Pearl Harbor. When Germany declared war on the United States three days later (December 11, 1941), Congress reciprocated. The U.S. Congress declared war on Axis allies

Bulgaria, Hungary, and Romania on June 4, 1942. Since then, the United States has been engaged in numerous militarized disputes, but no formally declared wars. The clause of the Constitution that James Madison believed to be the most important has not been invoked in over 75 years.

There were other major departures from the Constitution and traditional American approaches to the use of force after World War II. In particular, three big lessons drawn from the first and second world wars cast a long shadow over the conduct of U.S. foreign policy: the need for a dominant power to enforce global norms, the belief in trade and economic development as an engine for peace, and the conviction that all aggressors must be blocked and never "appeased."

Hegemonic Stability

In his book *War and Change in International Politics*, Robert Gilpin argues that major states will seek to alter the international system if "the expected benefits exceed the expected costs."[6] A single dominant state can raise the costs of changing the status quo. A wise and magnanimous hegemon can reduce other states' incentives for wanting to do so. If the status quo under the dominant power generally serves the interests of would-be challengers, the challengers may not bother.

As World War II ended, many U.S. leaders became convinced that the United States could and must be that single hegemon. They saw that in the 1920s and early 1930s, many countries were desperate to avoid a repeat of World War I. They negotiated arms-control agreements such as the Washington Naval

Treaties and the Kellogg–Briand Pact, which outlawed war. But in the eyes of many postwar observers, the United States' refusal to participate in the League of Nations doomed it to failure. High-minded notions of self-determination and the right to noninterference were worthless in the eyes of Germany's Adolf Hitler, Italy's Benito Mussolini, and Imperial Japan's ruling class. The United States should have been there, many argued, to stiffen other democracies' resolve.

A few Americans had a different perspective. For example, Charles Evans Hughes, who served as secretary of state from 1921 to 1925, doubted years later that formal U.S. membership in the league would have been sufficient to convince a reluctant public—both in the United States and Europe—to initiate a war. Surveying the belated and inadequate response to Germany's rearmament in violation of its treaty obligations, and its subsequent annexations and aggression, Hughes noted that "European powers could easily have stopped [Hitler] but they did not. . . . Neither Great Britain nor France wished war." He went on:

> Can any well-informed person, who looks at the matter realistically, believe that we should have taken a different view and as a member of the League would have thrown our weight against the policy of Great Britain and France, insisting on military action? They were immediately concerned and they, not we, had the military power to hold Hitler in check before it was too late. But they did not desire to use that power.[7]

Hughes conceded that a U.S. presence in some form would have enabled cooperation on a range of matters, and he anticipated that the postwar period would welcome an institution that could perform that function on a regular basis. But he cautioned against seeing such institutions as sufficient for ensuring the peace. "When it comes to the use of force," Hughes wrote, "the Great Powers . . . will act or fail to act" as their respective interests dictate. "Formal international organization will provide a useful mechanism to facilitate united action in the interest of peace but will not insure [sic] that action."[8]

The international organization created in the waning days of World War II reflected this essential insight. Rather than trusting in norms and good judgement, the United Nations accorded a privileged place to five permanent members of a Security Council that would decide on the critical matters of war and peace.

Within this framework, the United States performed an outsized role by virtue of its prodigious military and economic power. In subsequent years, American leaders would work through the United Nations when it suited them but skirt the institution when they deemed it more convenient to go it alone.

Economic Interdependence, Trade, and Peace

A second critical component of the postwar order was an open trading system. As with security, however, several observers argued that a single dominant power would need to keep it open. The United States assumed this role in the post–World War II era, serving as a market for goods and providing a stable currency for exchange and reserve.

First, some background. For much of recorded history, the leading cause of conflict was greed or avarice. At a most basic level, Thomas Hobbes recounts in *Leviathan*, men "use violence, to make themselves masters of other men's persons, wives, children, and cattle."[9] Great empires grew by conquest, seizing land, booty, and slaves from those they conquered. Strong and stable communities might be able to defend themselves from predators and grow their wealth slowly and steadily. But all of this hard work could be undone in an instant if a stronger and more powerful adversary appeared and took it all away by force—thus the constant need for defense. And when plagues or famines decimated one society's population or food stocks, even the most defensive minded could turn on a dime to become predators in their own right.

This pattern of seizing a new territory to grow one's wealth or to deny it to enemies reached its apotheosis in the 18th and 19th centuries. European countries scrambled to secure claims on every continent. The Spanish, French, and British vied for territories in the Western Hemisphere, Africa, and Asia. Even relatively small countries got in the game, the Dutch and the Portuguese establishing outposts in Africa and Asia as well as North and South America.

European rulers hoped to secure favorable arrangements for trade, including preferential access to raw materials and privileges for domestic producers. Within these regulated trading blocs, the dominant power could dictate terms for others wishing to do business there.

But a new generation of Enlightenment philosophers imagined a different set of arrangements, whereby countries grew wealthy not by conquest or by denying their adversaries' access to goods, but rather by affirming the rights of all civilized nations to trade freely. In the span of a few hundred years, trade went from being seen as a cause for war to a hoped-for cause for peace.

For example, Montesquieu imagined that just as commerce between individuals fostered virtuous behavior, so too would commerce between states "cure . . . the most destructive prejudices." The benefits were mutually reinforcing. "Wherever we find agreeable manners, there commerce flourishes," he wrote in the 20th book of his *Spirit of the Laws*, "and . . . wherever there is commerce, there we meet with agreeable manners." Agreeable manners, in turn, facilitated peace between nations. Thus, Montesquieu concluded, "the natural effect of commerce is to bring peace."[10]

Immanuel Kant agreed. "It is the spirit of trade," he wrote, "which cannot coexist with war, [and] which will, sooner or later, take hold of every people."[11]

By the mid-19th century, such ideas had spread widely. British intellectuals and politicians—including especially Richard Cobden and John Bright, the leaders of the Anti-Corn Law League—took up the cause of trade as a force for peace. Cobden spoke of free trade as "drawing men together, thrusting aside the antagonisms of race, and creeds and language, and uniting us in the bonds of eternal peace." He predicted that trade would cause the desire for empire to wither and for mighty militaries to "die away . . . when man becomes one family, and freely exchanges the fruits of his labor with his brother man."[12]

John Stuart Mill argued in 1848 that "commerce [was] rapidly rendering war obsolete." In his *Principles of Political Economy*, Mill wrote, "It may be said without exaggeration that the great extent and rapid increase of international trade, in being the principal guarantee of the peace of the world, is the great permanent security for the uninterrupted progress of the ideas, the institutions, and the character of the human race."[13]

Alas, the confident predictions that commerce would render war obsolete seem hopelessly naive when juxtaposed against the human carnage that occurred during the first half of the 20th century.

Perhaps no one felt this more acutely than the British journalist Norman Angell. In 1909, Angell published a pamphlet entitled *Europe's Optical Illusion*, which he later expanded into a book purporting to prove the link between trade and peace. Borrowing heavily from the insights of the Enlightenment thinkers profiled above, Angell's book *The Great Illusion* clarified their sweeping claims. Rather than arguing that trade made war obsolete, Angell argued that war—especially war between the industrial nations of Europe—was foolish and futile. Outright conquest would not generate sufficient economic gains for the conqueror to justify the expense, not to mention the risks to lives and property.

In earlier eras, war could generate considerable benefits, especially when the things worth acquiring were tangible and finite resources such as gold or land.[14] The process of wealth creation had evolved over the course of human history, however. By the early 20th century, it was founded on ready access to credit and capital, and the ability to take advantage of divisions of labor and economic specialization to generate mutually beneficial exchanges for all parties. In fact, in this new era, wars were more likely to make states poorer, not richer, as conflict would not only cost lives and money but also disrupt the bonds of trust and cooperation that had been built over many decades.

In short, extensive trade among nations seemed to have turned the old maxim of conquest for gain on its head. The "great illusion" was that nations achieved greatness through war. Trade now generated comparable benefits, at far less cost. Conversely, trade appeared to create interdependencies between states that raised the costs of war.

But the simple fact that Germany had possessed extensive trading relations with both Great Britain and France on the eve of World War I cast doubt on whether commerce was as pacifying as 19th-century liberals hoped.

Those doubts persisted during the interwar period. The punitive terms imposed on Germany after World War I devastated the German economy and impeded postwar trade among the former belligerents. Hyperinflation washed away household savings, only deepening the German public's despair. These conditions proved fertile ground for the extreme political movements that pledged to reverse the Versailles Treaty. Adolf Hitler's National Socialists didn't stop there: they promised to create a Third Reich, restore Germany to greatness, and wreak vengeance on enemies both foreign (especially France) and domestic (e.g., Jews, Roma, and communists).

The British economist John Maynard Keynes anticipated some of this. He had witnessed the treaty negotiations as a representative of David Lloyd George's government at the Paris Peace Conference, and he resigned in protest over what he characterized as a "Carthaginian" (i.e., overly punitive) peace. His *Economic Consequences of the Peace* surveyed the terms of the Versailles Treaty before the ink had even dried, warning that depriving Germany of its commercial and industrial infrastructure would lead to disaster, and not merely for the defeated Germans.

Germany was compelled to pay reparations, which reduced the amount of money available for the purchase of foreign goods. The Versailles Treaty also significantly restricted Germany's most important exports and industries, which further undermined the German economy. Trade between Germany and its three main World War I foes—England, France, and Italy—never recovered to prewar levels. Deepening resentment over debts paid and unpaid whipped up nationalist sentiment in many European countries.

Although U.S. leaders opposed some of the more punitive elements of the Versailles Treaty and helped negotiate sorely needed debt restructuring in the 1920s (the Dawes Plan and Dawes Commission), Americans also contributed to the breakdown of the international economy by embracing their own protectionist, illiberal trade policies. The Smoot–Hawley Tariff was the most notorious of several beggar-thy-neighbor measures that stifled foreign trade and choked off economic recovery after the stock-market crash of 1929.

Determined not to repeat these errors in the post–World War II order, the United States convened a meeting of finance ministers and leading economists at the Bretton Woods resort in New Hampshire in 1944. Out of that meeting emerged a set of economic institutions, including the International Bank for

Reconstruction and Development (i.e., the World Bank) and the International Monetary Fund, which would provide liquidity in sluggish times and stabilize global currencies with U.S. dollars backed by gold. Separately, U.S. officials pushed a series of multilateral trade negotiations—the General Agreement on Tariffs and Trade (GATT)—that they hoped would counteract the world's worst protectionist instincts. All told, eight separate GATT rounds significantly reduced tariffs and trade barriers in the decades after World War II. The World Trade Organization effectively supplanted the GATT in 1995.

European leaders learned lessons as well. Although the Soviets extracted massive economic concessions from the parts of Eastern Europe that fell under the sway of the Red Army—especially East Germany—the leaders of Western Europe opted for a different approach. They focused on expanding economic ties, facilitating recovery, and hopefully forestalling the rise of nationalism and authoritarianism as had occurred in Germany and Italy after World War I. French politician Robert Schuman first had the idea of bringing together Europe's coal and steel producers and consumers by reducing or removing national trade barriers. The Schuman Plan became the European Coal and Steel Community (composed of France, West Germany, Italy, Belgium, the Netherlands, and Luxembourg), which evolved into the European Economic Community (and eventually the European Union as we know it today).

Trade had failed to stop the first world war, and protectionism had exacerbated the nationalist tensions that gave rise to the second. A combination of new economic institutions and expanded trade, the post–World War II generation hoped, would forestall World War III.

Confront, Don't Appease, Aggressors

With the benefit of hindsight, many believe that the deal struck at Munich in September 1938 between British prime minister Neville Chamberlain and German chancellor Adolf Hitler ranks as among the worst diplomatic agreements in history. Believing that the handover of the Sudetenland in Czechoslovakia would satiate Hitler's appetite for expansion, Chamberlain famously declared that the Munich Agreement ensured "peace for our time." He was wrong. Within months of the deal, Hitler's Germany had devoured most parts of Czechoslovakia not handed over at Munich. And six months later, he had attacked Poland, a British ally. By September 1939, less than one year after the Munich Agreement was signed, England and Germany were at war.

Ever since, American presidents and foreign policy experts have pointed to this episode—and similar cases during the interwar period, including the Japanese invasion and occupation of Manchuria in 1931 and Benito Mussolini's assaults on Abyssinia (modern-day Ethiopia) in 1935—as proof positive that rapacious dictators should never be appeased and that aggression must always be met with force. Oftentimes, this equates to seeing any concessions in negotiations—or even diplomacy itself—as naive, reckless, and dangerous.

For many of the harshest critics of the Munich Agreement, the particulars are immaterial. There is reason to believe, however, that Adolf Hitler was a unique phenomenon in human history: a megalomaniacal leader in control of a powerful state and capable of carrying out his most evil desires. Meanwhile, though it may be true that, in retrospect, Chamberlain erred in negotiating with Hitler, it does not follow that any and every other leader should always choose war over peace. Even Winston Churchill, one of Chamberlain's harshest critics, later admitted that "appeasement in itself may be good or bad according to the circumstances."[15]

Be that as it may, many U.S. leaders who came of age during the 1930s and World War II approached the deepening Cold War with the Soviet Union with a single model in mind: it was always 1938, and every other tin-pot tyrant was the next Hitler. In practice, this typically entailed U.S. policymakers' portraying relatively small and remote places as merely the first volley in a plan for Soviet domination of a particular region and thus the spark that would ignite an inevitable global conflict.

For example, when Russia threatened to leave troops in the northern Iranian province of Azerbaijan after the end of World War II, the Iranian ambassador to Washington pleaded for help. If the Russians' plans were not thwarted, he warned, the "history of Manchuria, Abyssinia, and Munich would be repeated and Azerbaijan would prove to have been [the] first shot fired in [the] third world war."[16]

Turkey was similarly vulnerable, and it might have served as a convenient avenue for Soviet domination of the entire Middle East. "There isn't a doubt in my mind," President Harry Truman confided in a longhand letter to Secretary of State James Byrnes, "that Russia intends an invasion of Turkey and the seizure of the Black Sea Straits to the Mediterranean. Unless Russia is faced with an iron fist and strong language, another war is in the making."[17]

Thus, explains the renowned diplomatic historian Ernest May, "Truman and his advisers felt impelled to resist the 'totalitarian' Soviet Union now, before its appetite fed upon itself, Soviet power increased, and the people of the United States and other countries faced a Moloch more horrible than those to which so many lives had so recently been sacrificed."[18]

And in June 1950, when North Korea's Kim Il Sung sent troops south across the 38th parallel, Truman responded with force. Before the incident, the National Security Council (NSC), with Truman in the chair, had concluded that "Korea is of little strategic value to the United States and that any commitment to United States use of military force in Korea would be ill-advised."[19]

After Kim's aggression, however, Truman's perspective changed. "In my generation," he later wrote,

> this was not the first occasion when the strong had attacked the weak. I recalled some earlier instances: Manchuria, Ethiopia, Austria. I remembered how each time that the democracies failed to act it had encouraged the aggressors to keep going ahead. Communism was acting in Korea just as Hitler, Mussolini, and the Japanese had acted ten, fifteen, and twenty years earlier. . . . If this was allowed to go unchallenged it would mean a third world war, just as similar incidents had brought on the second world war.[20]

In the ensuing years of the Cold War, U.S. policymakers justified U.S. intervention to shore up states threatened from without and within—from Guatemala and Iran to Vietnam and Lebanon—on similar grounds. Today we call it the domino theory. It marked a striking departure from prewar U.S. history, when U.S. presidents scrupulously avoided foreign entanglements. Now virtually any place, no matter how remote, could be portrayed as strategically vital. The presumption concerning U.S. military intervention shifted from "Why?" to "Why not?"

And as the United States retained and perfected the power to intervene militarily in distant disputes, this precipitated a critical change in the U.S. economy and a concomitant transformation in U.S. politics. We turn to the growth of the military-industrial complex in the next chapter.

6

The Permanent Warfare State

The U.S. Constitution stipulated that the federal government would maintain a navy, but it directed that armies be raised as necessary and that no funds for such a force be appropriated for more than two years. If the country's leaders were determined to prosecute a long war, the nation's founding document compelled them to return regularly to the American people for money and support.

The Founders had hoped to avoid, in the words of George Washington, the "overgrown military establishments" that characterized the European empires of their era. Nearly 200 years later, another revered military leader turned politician worried aloud that the old model might be gone for good.

In his farewell address, delivered from the Oval Office on January 17, 1961, Dwight David Eisenhower explained:

> Until the latest of our world conflicts, the United States had no armaments industry. American makers of plowshares could, with time and as required, make swords as well. But now we can no longer risk emergency improvisation of national defense; we have been compelled to create a permanent armaments industry of vast proportions. . . .
>
> This conjunction of an immense military establishment and a large arms industry is new in the American experience. The total influence—economic, political, even spiritual—is felt in every city, every State house, every office of the Federal government. We recognize the imperative need for this development. Yet we must not fail to comprehend its grave implications. Our toil, resources and livelihood are all involved; so is the very structure of our society.[1]

Eisenhower rarely doubted the need for a strong military establishment in order to compete with, face down, and eventually prevail over the Soviet Union and its communist allies. But he worried constantly about the impact that a decades-long struggle would have on the institutions of government inside the United States. And yet despite his popularity and his demonstrated expertise in all things related to the military and security, Eisenhower was unable to stem the cries to do more. World War II had changed Americans' attitudes toward standing armies and a permanent peacetime military establishment, and the Cold War effectively finished the transformation. By the time the Cold War ended, with the fall of the Berlin Wall in November 1989 and the dissolution of the Soviet Union two years later, America's military establishment had become a permanent fixture in the country's political, economic, and even cultural life.

This chapter discusses how it happened.

* * *

During the world wars, Americans managed to escape some of the worst excesses of what the sociologist Harold D. Lasswell had called "the garrison state."[2] Although they tolerated countless small—and a few not-so-small—infringements on their individual liberty as necessary for waging war, most of the essential elements of a functioning democracy endured during the course of both conflicts. Politicians still had to run for election and reelection. Men and women on the home front chafed at rationing, and wage and price controls, but these hardly compared to the privation and suffering endured by hundreds of millions of men and women living in the Soviet Union, Japanese-occupied China, the islands of the South Pacific, or Nazi-controlled Europe. For the most part, those in office were compelled to abide by the laws of the land. Meanwhile, most Americans had it pretty good, and U.S. industry boomed.

Not everyone in the United States fared well, however. Over 100,000 Japanese Americans were unjustly imprisoned during World War II, an incident made only more horrible by the Supreme Court's decision to sanction such an action as consistent with the

Constitution. This was a reminder that war could upend—at least temporarily—even the nation's most sacred principles. As with other great crises in American history, the government *did* expand its influence considerably and not always at the expense of corporate interests. But while war was good for *some* businesses, that didn't mean that it was good for *most* businesses or for consumers. As Robert Higgs explains in *Crisis and Leviathan*, beginning prior to World War I, various interest groups pushed the U.S. economy from something like laissez faire capitalism to a mixed economy with room for crony capitalism and rampant rent-seeking.[3] During wartime, business leaders often collaborated with government to direct and control industries deemed vital to the war effort. In practice, such corporatism pushed war costs onto other less-well-represented persons and groups. The Supreme Court also sanctified the steady erosion of individual rights during wartime, and it rarely restored the prewar balance when the shooting stopped and the nation returned to supposed normalcy.

Meanwhile, some Americans paid a higher price than others did. Of the 4.8 million persons who served in World War I, nearly 2.8 million were draftees. That all occurred after a formal declaration of war in April 1917. The first peacetime draft in the nation's history, the Selective Training and Service Act, was enacted into law on September 16, 1940, and exposed tens of millions to the threat of forced service. "Of the sixteen million who served in the armed forces during [WWII]," notes Higgs, "ten million were conscripts. . . . Further many of the volunteers came forward only because of the draft, some seeking to avoid the uncomfortable and dangerous service in the infantry by joining the Navy."[4]

Dissenters and conscientious objectors were also exposed to harassment, both legal and extralegal. Some of the more notorious cases occurred during World War I, when the Espionage and Sedition Acts subjected over 2,000 people to criminal prosecution for daring to express their views. The Wilson administration, notes Cato senior fellow Ted Galen Carpenter, "co-opted most elements of the press as part of a massive propaganda campaign to 'sell' the war effort to the American people, and critics who would not be co-opted were intimidated or suppressed."[5]

For example, socialist leader Eugene V. Debs was sentenced to a 10-year prison term for a speech in Canton, Ohio, in which he voiced skepticism about the war. Movie producer Robert Goldstein received a similarly harsh 10-year prison sentence for making a film about the American Revolution. The reason? The government was concerned that the film, which depicted British atrocities during the Revolution, "incited hostility" against an ally in the current conflict.[6] "For the first time in American history," Carpenter observes, "the government claimed a legal and moral right to exercise monopoly power over information on international affairs."[7]

"The worst legacy of the U.S. experience in World War I," Carpenter concludes, "was not restrictive legislation or even the public hysteria that made patriotism synonymous with intolerance. It was the willingness of both government officials and the public to abandon the commitment to long-standing fundamental liberties for the pursuit of foreign policy objectives."[8]

The atmosphere was quite different during World War II. Excepting the egregious internment of Japanese Americans, the federal government's efforts at stifling dissent were less blatant and heavy-handed than in World War I, though the net effect on individual liberty was no less insidious. During the wars, few questioned the state's authority to limit individual and press freedoms. And few challenged the efficacy of central planning. In short, the country that emerged from World War I and II was very different from the America of the 1900s and 1930s. And the transformation, including the steady growth of federal government power, continued even after most of the troops came home.

The Early Cold War

The dawning of the nuclear age cast a particularly long and ominous cloud over the American psyche. A people long accustomed to near imperviousness to foreign threats suddenly felt very vulnerable. Although their cities had survived the war unscathed, the advent of air power, and later long-range strategic bombing, sowed doubts about whether the United States' peculiar geography continued to bestow great benefits. Urban bomb shelters and air raid sirens, used only in civil defense drills in the early 1940s, seemed wholly inadequate against the destructive power of atomic, and then thermonuclear, weapons. As the Cold War deepened, Americans were prepared to tolerate—and often demanded—draconian security measures, measures that they had avoided during all previous wars. Some wondered if the republic could survive under the shadow of Armageddon.

And if the public didn't seem sufficiently alarmed, political leaders were more than happy to frighten them. When Harry Truman was thinking of ways to rally the American people to fight the nascent Cold War, he turned to his former senator colleagues for advice. Michigan senator Arthur Vandenberg, chairman of the Foreign Relations Committee, advised Truman to "make a personal appearance before Congress and scare the hell out of the American people."[9] Dean Acheson, Truman's secretary of state, would later explain that they painted a picture of the global communist menace that was "clearer than truth."[10]

NSC 68, a classified document prepared for the National Security Council in early 1950, reflected the prevailing mood among some of Truman's most-senior foreign policy advisors at the time. Truman initially resisted NSC 68's darkly pessimistic tone, as well as its call for massive military-spending increases. But the shock of Korea, coupled with the victory of the Chinese communists and advances in the Soviet nuclear program, changed his mind. Furthermore, when the initial defense-spending increase to fight the Korean War did not create obvious economic hardship, Truman faced little public resistance to further spending increases. He approved NSC 68 as official policy in September 1950.

By then, Truman had come to equate U.S. national security with a stronger U.S. military—one that could confront and deter Soviet aggression directly, virtually anywhere it might emerge. North Korea's invasion of the South seemed to confirm the Truman administration's view of bad Soviet intentions. NSC 68 asserted, "The Soviet Union . . . is animated by a new fanatic faith, antithetical to our own, and seeks to impose its absolute authority over the rest of the world." This led the authors to conclude that "the risks we face are of a new order of magnitude, commensurate with the total struggle in which we are engaged. . . . These risks crowd in on us, in a shrinking world of polarized power, so as to give us no choice, ultimately, between meeting them effectively or being overcome by them."[11]

In this sense, increasing the size of the military seemed like a natural progression with few domestic consequences. "The United States could achieve a substantial absolute increase in output," NSC 68 explained, "and could thereby increase the allocation of resources to a build-up of the economic and military strength of itself and its allies without suffering a decline in its real standard of living."[12] Believing that any government spending contributes to economic growth, NSC 68 viewed guns *and* butter as the key to long-term prosperity.

In short, NSC 68 provided the intellectual groundwork for the permanent warfare state. Princeton's Aaron Friedberg writes: "NSC 68 was, in essence, a battering ram with which its authors hoped to shatter the existing budget ceiling."[13] Though the document remained classified for decades, government officials disseminated the underlying ideas widely. One might further say that, in conjunction with all the other national security reforms of the late 1940s and early 1950s, NSC 68 also shattered any further resistance to a large and permanent military. When the Truman administration came up with an estimate for the cost of its military proposals after the outbreak of war in Korea, it called for a defense budget of as much as $40 billion, an increase of nearly 300 percent. A follow-on study approved on Truman's last day in office, January 19, 1953, reaffirmed NSC 68's basic arguments, including the need for—and possible advantages of—substantial military spending to boost the economy.

Eisenhower's Fight with the Military-Industrial Complex

Dwight David Eisenhower was uniquely qualified to ponder the implications of the changing nature of warfare and what it meant for the American economy and American democracy. Freshly graduated from the U.S. Military Academy at West Point, Eisenhower was commissioned as an officer in the U.S. Army in 1915. A handful of his classmates saw action in Europe during World War I but, much to his chagrin, Eisenhower missed his chance. He gained respect as an able staff assistant for better-known officers such as Douglas MacArthur, but never any fame.

World War II changed all that. Compelled to perform multiple roles as Supreme Allied Commander in Europe—equal parts military strategist, diplomat, and politician—Eisenhower emerged from the conflict as one of the most revered figures in American history. He became one of only five U.S. Army officers to ever pin on a fifth star.

Harry Truman tried to convince him to run for president in 1948 as a Democrat and even offered to step aside if the general said yes. But Ike demurred. Instead he bided his time, first as president of Columbia University and then as the first Supreme Allied Commander of the newly formed North Atlantic Treaty Organization, before declaring his candidacy for the Republican nomination in 1952.

He beat back a primary challenge from Ohio senator Robert Taft and then defeated Illinois senator Adlai Stevenson in the general election. As the first Republican elected to the office in 20 years, it wasn't exactly a cakewalk. But Americans were anxious about the Cold War and frustrated by the "police action" in far-off Korea that had become a grinding stalemate. Eisenhower pledged to go to Korea personally, which many voters interpreted as a promise to fix the Korea problem. And if he could do that, who was to say that a breakthrough in the tense Cold War was impossible?

When Eisenhower entered the Oval Office in January 1953, he confronted an interlocking set of challenges. In addition to the war raging in Korea, there was the standoff with the Soviet Union in Europe, Communist Chinese threats against the United States' Nationalist Chinese allies in Taiwan, and the slow but inexorable decline of America's allies, especially Great Britain and France, as they struggled to hold on to the remnants of their colonial empires. British abandonment of Greece prompted Truman to pledge to use U.S. diplomatic, economic, and even military support to protect free nations, either from external forces or from insurgent movements within. Eisenhower was afforded a chance to intervene in Vietnam, a former French colony, but in 1954 he refused to commit to a massive effort to rescue the besieged French garrison at Dien Bien Phu. He likewise resisted calls to intervene publicly and decisively in the Suez and Hungary crises in 1956, opting instead for covert interventions in places like Iran in 1953 and Guatemala in 1954.[14]

Two factors explain Eisenhower's relative caution. The first was his sincere belief that small-scale, conventional conflicts could easily spiral into large-scale, nuclear ones. And there could be no victory in a thermonuclear war—of that Eisenhower was certain. When asked what to do in the event of such a war with the Soviet Union, Eisenhower replied, "You might as well go out and shoot everyone you see and then shoot yourself."[15] On another occasion, Eisenhower tamped down calls for a massive civil defense program or an even more urgent nuclear buildup to ensure that the United States could prevail in such a contest. "You just can't have this kind of war," he said. "There aren't enough bulldozers to scrape the bodies off the streets."[16]

But while a thermonuclear exchange was unthinkable, a decades-long conflict characterized by massive mobilization and huge military expenditures wasn't very appealing either.

When he entered office in January 1953, Eisenhower inherited a budget from the outgoing Truman administration that called for spending 14.2 percent of GDP on the military. In real dollar terms, U.S. military spending had more than tripled between 1950 and 1952. Some of Truman's advisers believed that this wasn't nearly enough. Eisenhower considered that amount to be intolerably high, even though it was hardly unprecedented: spending during World War II surpassed 37 percent of GDP in 1944. Had Eisenhower asked the American people to undertake a similar effort, they likely would have gone along. Instead, he opted for a different approach.

In a speech before the American Society of Newspaper Editors at the Statler Hotel in Washington, DC, Eisenhower explained what the deepening Cold War could mean for Americans, and for the world.

Delivered in April 1953—a few weeks after the death of Soviet leader Joseph Stalin—and broadcast on television and radio, the dark and foreboding speech contained a kernel of optimism. He hoped that new leadership in the Soviet Union would reciprocate his expressions of goodwill and would welcome his stated desire for peace. If they did not, Eisenhower warned, the consequences would be grim.

The best and worst cases "can be simply stated," he said.

"The worst is atomic war."

"The best," he went on, "would be this: a life of perpetual fear and tension; a burden of arms draining the wealth and the labor of all peoples; a wasting of strength that defies the American system or the Soviet system or any system to achieve true abundance and happiness for the peoples of this earth."

He then spelled out the tradeoffs that Americans would be forced to endure in order to sustain a massive military undertaking. These were the opportunity costs, the things that Americans would be compelled to forego if the contest with the Soviet Union could not be reined in:

> Every gun that is made, every warship launched, every rocket fired signifies, in the final sense, a theft from those who hunger and are not fed, those who are cold and are not clothed.
>
> This world in arms is not spending money alone. It is spending the sweat of its laborers, the genius of its scientists, the hopes of its children.
>
> The cost of one modern heavy bomber is this: a modern brick school in more than 30 cities.
>
> It is two electric power plants, each serving a town of 60,000 population.
>
> It is two fine, fully equipped hospitals. It is some 50 miles of concrete highway.

We pay for a single fighter plane with a half million bushels of wheat.

We pay for a single destroyer with new homes that could have housed more than 8,000 people.

This, I repeat, is the best way of life to be found on the road the world has been taking.

This is not a way of life at all, in any true sense. Under the cloud of threatening war, it is humanity hanging from a cross of iron.[17]

In his "Chance for Peace" speech (glass-half-empty scholars prefer to call it the "Cross of Iron" speech), Eisenhower presented the opportunity costs associated with an open-ended militarized standoff. He hoped to avert a deepening Cold War or, failing that, to control its costs. In the ensuing eight years, Eisenhower strove to strike a balance between the need to deter the Soviet Union from any aggressive designs it might have, in Europe or elsewhere, and the need to protect the U.S. economy from fiscal collapse.

For Eisenhower, military expenditures were a necessary evil, and excessive military expenditures were inherently wasteful and unproductive. The true source of the United States' strength, and the key to its ability to eventually prevail over the Soviet Union, was a healthy U.S. economy. Thus, an escalating arms race that diverted resources out of the most productive sectors of the economy would be detrimental; in effect, it would hand a victory to the Soviets without their having to fire a shot.

Although he had lived nearly his entire adult life in uniform, Eisenhower had long harbored doubts about the intrinsic value of military spending, and he was particularly skeptical of tighter coordination between the military and the private sector. But he was also skeptical of the claims that war profiteering and the "merchants of death" had driven the country into an ill-advised war in 1917.

In 1930 and 1931, the army assigned Eisenhower, a major at the time, to study industrial mobilization for the War Policies Commission, a panel created by Congress to explore the relationship between profit and war.

Some in Congress, including especially North Dakota senator Gerald Nye, believed that "the removal of the element of profit from war would materially remove the danger of more war."[18]

Eisenhower doubted that this was true. He also recognized that separating profits from military industry would be detrimental to efficiency and corrosive to American values. To Eisenhower, the nationalization of private industries could only be justified in cases of dire national emergency. It would be unconscionable during peacetime.

Instead, Eisenhower aimed for balance. He worried that a failure to reconcile the nation's means (resources, public will) and ends (strategic goals) would pose as great a security threat as the Soviet menace.

In 1947, for example, he confided in a letter to his friend Walter Bedell "Beetle" Smith that "the annual expenditure of unconscionable sums on a [defense] program of indefinite duration, extending far into the future," could be disastrous for the U.S. economy. Strategists must recognize that "national security and national solvency are mutually dependent," and they must craft policies accordingly. If they did not, he warned, the U.S. economy could collapse under the "crushing weight of military power."[19]

Eisenhower returned to this theme repeatedly. During testimony before Congress in 1951, he stressed that the U.S. system "must remain solvent, as we attempt a solution to this great problem of security. Else we have lost the battle from within that we are trying to win from without."[20] In his first State of the Union address as president, delivered before a joint session of Congress on February 2, 1953, he explained: "Our problem is to achieve adequate military strength within the limits of endurable strain upon our economy. To amass military power without regard to our economic capacity would be to defend ourselves against one kind of disaster by inviting another."[21]

Eisenhower had in mind a "great equation" that defined a nation's military and fiscal health. If the burden of providing the armaments and manpower to prosecute the Cold War grew too high, it would do grave damage. "Spiritual force, multiplied by economic force, multiplied by military force is roughly equal to security. . . . If one of these factors falls to zero, or near zero, the resulting product does likewise."[22]

In the ensuing eight years, Eisenhower gained an even greater appreciation for how perpetual war was changing the nature of the American state and, ultimately, America itself. He battled military leaders, including many of his former army colleagues, who objected to his strategy of massive retaliation. He dealt with hawkish Democrats in Congress, including Senate Majority Leader Lyndon Johnson, Washington's Sen. Henry M. "Scoop"

Jackson, Missourian Stuart Symington (a former secretary of the U.S. Air Force), and a young John F. Kennedy from Massachusetts, who accused him of downplaying the Soviet threat. He parried Keynesian economists who disdained his fiscal conservatism and who alleged that his conventional thinking was both forcing the United States to fight with one hand behind its back and preventing the U.S. economy from reaching its full potential. He even endured at least two heart attacks.

But he survived, as did the nation. The worst possible outcome—nuclear war—was averted. And while military spending as a share of GDP far exceeded levels seen before World War II, it seems apparent that spending would have been even higher had it not been for Eisenhower's determination to contain costs and to craft a grand strategy that was mindful of the tradeoffs.

Surveying the state of the nation at the end of his second term, Eisenhower had mixed emotions. Although Eisenhower remained popular with the American people, Kennedy's victory in the 1960 presidential election over Richard Nixon, Eisenhower's vice president, was partly a repudiation of Eisenhower's conduct of the Cold War. Kennedy's campaign rhetoric spoke of getting the country moving again, calling attention to the looming gap between a seemingly rising, emboldened Soviet Union and a tired, complacent United States.

In his parting words as president, Eisenhower tried to put into context the geopolitical situation that his successor would inherit. In the process, he hearkened back to some of the same themes that he had invoked eight years earlier in his "Chance for Peace" speech. Above all, he implored his fellow citizens to take an active interest in balancing the nation's security needs with its long-term fiscal and spiritual health:

> Throughout America's adventure in free government, our basic purposes have been to keep the peace; to foster progress in human achievement, and to enhance liberty, dignity and integrity among people and among nations. . . .
>
> Progress toward these noble goals is persistently threatened by the conflict now engulfing the world. It commands our whole attention, absorbs our very beings. We face a hostile ideology—global in scope, atheistic in character, ruthless in purpose, and insidious in method. Unhappily the danger it poses promises to be of indefinite duration. To meet it successfully, there is called for, not so much the emotional and transitory sacrifices of crisis, but rather those which enable us to carry forward steadily, surely, and without complaint the burdens of a prolonged and complex struggle—with liberty the stake. Only thus shall we remain, despite every provocation, on our charted course toward permanent peace and human betterment.
>
> Crises there will continue to be. In meeting them, whether foreign or domestic, great or small, there is a recurring temptation to feel that some spectacular and costly action could become the miraculous solution to all current difficulties. A huge increase in newer elements of our defense; development of unrealistic programs to cure every ill in agriculture; a dramatic expansion in basic

and applied research—these and many other possibilities, each possibly promising in itself, may be suggested as the only way to the road we wish to travel.

But each proposal must be weighed in the light of a broader consideration: the need to maintain balance in and among national programs—balance between the private and the public economy, balance between cost and hoped for advantage—balance between the clearly necessary and the comfortably desirable; balance between our essential requirements as a nation and the duties imposed by the nation upon the individual; balance between actions of the moment and the national welfare of the future. Good judgment seeks balance and progress; lack of it eventually finds imbalance and frustration.[23]

He closed with a few observations about the military that he knew so well. "A vital element in keeping the peace," he affirmed, "is our military establishment. Our arms must be mighty, ready for instant action, so that no potential aggressor may be tempted to risk his own destruction."

At the same time, however, he was anxious of how a permanent armaments industry represented a dramatic departure from the nation's traditions, and how it could pose a threat to the very system that the military was intended to protect and defend:

In the councils of government, we must guard against the acquisition of unwarranted influence, whether sought or unsought, by the military-industrial complex. The potential for the disastrous rise of misplaced power exists and will persist.

We must never let the weight of this combination endanger our liberties or democratic processes. We should take nothing for granted. Only an alert and knowledgeable citizenry can compel the proper meshing of the huge industrial and military machinery of defense with our peaceful methods and goals, so that security and liberty may prosper together.[24]

It was an incisive and profound speech by a man not known for his oratory skills. At the time, and for some years since, it was overshadowed by John F. Kennedy's inaugural address, delivered three days later. But today, Eisenhower's prudence and restraint is more likely to find favor among historians than JFK's pledge to "pay any price, bear any burden, meet any hardship, support any friend, [and] oppose any foe to assure the survival and the success of liberty."[25] The juxtaposition between Eisenhower's dour warning and Kennedy's unbridled optimism couldn't be more stark.

After all, Americans paid a steep price in lives and treasure in the 1960s under Kennedy and his successor Lyndon Johnson, and they bore many burdens. More than 58,000 names are memorialized in black granite on the National Mall. At least 300,000 of the 2.7 million military personnel who served in Vietnam were wounded, and many more bore scars too deep and hidden to have been officially counted.

By the early 1970s, many Americans began to question some of the anti-communist nostrums that had sustained U.S. foreign policy for over two decades. Images of suffering, oppression, and abuse undercut the argument that Americans were fighting to make life better for the Vietnamese people. That might have been the intention, but the reality was something quite different. After all, over 3 million Vietnamese died in the conflict, though the true scale was not obvious at the time. Within a few years, Americans would learn of other abuses perpetrated in the name of anti-communism around the world, from assassination plots in Cuba to various efforts to influence elections in foreign countries.

In light of the country's Vietnam War experience, it is unsurprising that the United States stepped back from waging foreign wars in the 1970s and early 1980s. The military shrank in size, from 3.5 million active duty in 1968 to just over 2 million in 1979, and shifted from a force composed chiefly of conscripts to a professional military staffed solely by men and women who chose to serve. The military shrunk again after the end of the Cold War, from 2.2 million in 1987 to less than 1.5 million in 2000. Spending fell to just under 3 percent of GDP by 1999.[26]

But in other respects, Eisenhower's warning of a permanent military-industrial complex proved prophetic. One might have expected the U.S. military to have shrunk even more, maybe even returning to its pre–Cold War and pre–World War II roots: a small standing force deployed chiefly in the United States, which could be augmented by reservists and other new recruits if conditions warranted.

Instead, political and economic interests—and sheer inertia—kept military spending relatively high despite the disappearance of the Soviet foe that the force was ostensibly designed to defeat.

In *The American Warfare State*, Rebecca Thorpe traces the growth and persistence of the military-industrial complex back to World War II. War production in new locales, especially the suburbs of major cities and the agricultural and underdeveloped areas in the South and West, created a durable political constituency that supported continued weapons production after the war's end. Those locales, and the people representing them in Congress, were also more likely to support U.S. involvement in foreign wars.[27]

Meanwhile, the "alert and knowledgeable citizenry" that Eisenhower hoped would ensure the continued coexistence of both liberty and security has given way to an executive branch with both the means and motive to wage war, and a Congress seemingly powerless to stop it.

This dynamic played out in the wars fought after the terrorist attacks of September 11, 2001.

7

Post-9/11:
Terrorizing Ourselves

During the Cold War, fear of communism convinced Americans to accept the creation of a permanent warfare state, something they had previously refused to do. After the Soviet Union collapsed, the warfare state remained, sustained mostly by inertia. And the U.S. military was busy in the years after the fall of the Berlin Wall: from major interventions like the First Gulf War in 1990–1991 to smaller operations in Panama (1989), Somalia (1992–1993), and the Balkans (1995–1996 and 1998–1999). Few of these missions, however, made Americans safer. Americans supported—or at least tolerated—such interventions if the costs were low and the intended object was noble. But such support was always fragile. Military missions that did not advance U.S. security or serve core U.S. national security interests were rarely deemed worthy of the loss of even a single American soldier.

All that changed after the horrible events of September 11, 2001. The public was hungry for vengeance abroad. Meanwhile, at home, fear of terrorism induced Americans to accept limitations on their freedoms and intrusions on their privacy that they had never tolerated before, not even during World Wars I and II or the Cold War that followed.

We have paid a heavy price in more tangible ways, too. At the federal level alone, the cost of counterterrorism measures exceeds $1 trillion. This includes terrorism-related increases at the FBI and the myriad intelligence agencies, and the creation of a new cabinet-level department, the Department of Homeland Security. State and local governments have spent many billions more. And the private sector has likely spent as much as the government on security measures—for example, the guards who check your ID when you enter an office building.

Fear of terrorism served as a rationale for two major wars launched after 9/11. The war against the Taliban government that had harbored al Qaeda in Afghanistan was a logical response to the attacks. It was important to disrupt the training camps there and put the group under unrelenting pressure. The need to send a message to other regimes that might have tolerated the presence of anti-American terror groups in their midst was also a key rationale.

But within hours of the attacks, a small but important group of Americans saw an opportunity to go after another target that they had kept in sight for years: Saddam Hussein's Iraq.

In 1997, *Weekly Standard* editor William Kristol and Robert Kagan of the Carnegie Endowment for International Peace founded the Project for the New American Century (PNAC), an organization dedicated to the belief "that American leadership is good both for America and for the world; and that such leadership requires military strength, diplomatic energy and commitment to moral principle."[1] The signatories to the organization's statement of principles included former vice president Dan Quayle (Kristol's one-time boss), publishers and pundits such as Steve Forbes and Norman Podhoretz, and a plethora of Ford, Reagan, and H. W. Bush administration officials, including Elliott Abrams, William Bennett, Donald Rumsfeld, and Paul Wolfowitz.[2]

In certain respects, PNAC's approach to the United States' role in the world hearkened back to Alfred Thayer Mahan and Theodore Roosevelt in the late 1800s, and *Time*'s Henry Luce and other early cold warriors at midcentury. But the organization was practically fixated from its earliest days on the Iraqi dictator. In January 1998, PNAC published its first open letter, calling on President Bill Clinton "to enunciate a new strategy that . . . should aim, above all, at the removal of Saddam Hussein's regime from power" by military means, if necessary.[3]

Kristol and Kagan coauthored op-eds in the *New York Times* and *Washington Post*, reiterating that Hussein was in possession of weapons of mass destruction and insisting that he must be removed by force.[4] Several months later, PNAC issued a second open letter reiterating its demand that Hussein be overthrown.[5]

This effort bore fruit in October 1998 when Congress passed the Iraq Liberation Act. The act committed the United States to regime change in Iraq as official policy, stipulating that opposition groups dedicated to Hussein's overthrow, and vetted by the U.S. government, would be entitled to American assistance.[6]

One of the leading recipients of U.S. aid was the Iraqi National Congress (INC). The INC's leader, Ahmed Chalabi, had been carefully cultivating allies in the United States for years. Despite such support, however, Chalabi's organization had utterly failed in its bid to topple Hussein's government. That pattern persisted after the passage of the Iraq Liberation Act. The INC's coffers were flooded with U.S. taxpayer cash, but Hussein remained firmly in power in Baghdad. It was only after the September 11 terrorist attacks that the mission to remove him by force gained new momentum.

This was odd, given that Iraq was not involved in the attacks—a key fact that the advocates for war worked diligently to obscure. At times, the misdirection crossed over into outright deception.

For example, on December 9, 2001, Vice President Dick Cheney appeared on the NBC program *Meet the Press*. Asked by host Tim Russert whether there was any information showing that "Iraq was involved in the September 11" attacks, Cheney mentioned "a report that's been pretty well confirmed" that 9/11 lead hijacker Mohammed Atta had met with the Iraqi intelligence service in Prague several months before the attacks.[7] In fact, the CIA had concluded that no such meeting occurred and had informed the White House accordingly.[8] Cheney chose to ignore the agency's findings and continued to peddle the tale.

A major source of false or misleading material on Iraq was Chalabi and the INC. He often funneled such information through Judith Miller, a reporter for the *New York Times*, who either published the stories under her own byline or passed them along to her colleagues at the *Times*. Patrick Tyler and John Tagliabue, for example, broke the Atta-in-Prague tale. Another account involved Arab fighters allegedly training to hijack airplanes at a camp near Salman Pak in Iraq. Chalabi later confided to Miller that he had planted both stories.

Chalabi relied on a too-credulous media because many in the intelligence community considered him to be a self-dealing charlatan. Marc Garlasco, an analyst at the Defense Intelligence Agency, explained: "We had INC constantly shoving crap at us. You know, they were providing information that they thought we wanted to hear. They were feeding the beast."[9]

When another INC-connected defector, Adnan Ihsan Saeed al-Haideri, came forward with serious allegations involving the extent of Saddam Hussein's nuclear-, chemical-, and biological-weapons programs, the CIA suspected he was lying. But al-Haideri's allegations made it into the mainstream courtesy of Judith Miller and the *Times*. Chalabi biographer Aram Roston notes: "The story splashed across the newspapers of the world like a can of paint. Reuters, the Associated Press, and other wire services picked it up. Newspapers from Australia to Austin, Texas, ran the story. Network news anchors read terse accounts of it."[10]

One of the more significant episodes involving phony evidence was Secretary of State Colin Powell's speech before the United Nations on February 4, 2003. Relying in part on a source nicknamed "Curveball," Powell alleged that Iraq had an active chemical-weapons program that it was concealing from the prying eyes of international inspectors.[11] As with the claims of Saddam's links to 9/11, however, these allegations proved false.

Although Ahmad Chalabi, the INC, and other self-interested Iraqi defectors and expatriates are responsible for the lies that they told, U.S. officials are responsible for believing them and for then using the phony or misleading stories to build support for a disastrous war. The effort was directed both at the public and at professionals inside government. "We were being asked to do things and make sure that justification was out there," explains John Brennan, then deputy director of the CIA.[12] Veteran CIA analyst Paul Pillar agrees that "a policy decision clearly had been made" and that intelligence was expected "to support that decision."[13]

All told, according to a report by minority staff at the House Committee on Government Reform, Bush administration officials made "237 misleading statements about the threat posed by Iraq." Those implicated included Bush, Cheney, and Powell, as well as Secretary of Defense Donald Rumsfeld and National Security Advisor Condoleezza Rice. "These statements," the report went on, "were made in 125 separate appearances, consisting of 40 speeches, 26 press conference and briefings, 53 interviews, 4 written statements, and 2 congressional testimonies." According to the committee report, at least 61 separate statements "misrepresented Iraq's ties to al-Qaeda."[14] A Senate investigation reached similar conclusions.[15]

In addition to the Bush administration's effort to demonize Iraq, several important books also contributed to the case for war. In 2002, the Brookings Institution's Kenneth Pollack published *The Threatening Storm*, in which he argued "the only prudent and realistic course of action left to the United States is to mount a full-scale invasion of Iraq to smash the Iraqi armed forces, depose Saddam's regime, and rid the country of weapons of mass destruction." Such an undertaking, Pollack insisted, would not be very costly to the United States. "It is unimaginable," he wrote, "that the United States would have to contribute hundreds of billions of dollars and highly unlikely that we would have to contribute even tens of billions of dollars." He even seemed to doubt that many U.S. troops would be killed or injured, pointing to the recent conflict in Bosnia in which U.S. forces "have not suffered a single casualty from hostile action because they have become so attentive and skillful at force protection."[16]

Then, in early 2003, PNAC's Kristol teamed up with Lawrence Kaplan, an editor at the left-leaning *New Republic*, to write *The War over Iraq*. Although mostly recycling claims that had already received a wide airing in public, Kristol and Kaplan—like Pollack before them—portrayed the costs of war with Iraq as modest and manageable.[17]

* * *

But while a bipartisan group of elected officials, think tank scholars, and journalists were working overtime to push the United States toward war with Iraq, a smaller but no-less-determined group of individuals was trying just as hard to stop it.

Much of this effort centered on a loose coalition of international relations scholars outside Washington, DC. Not privy to information that might have disproved the Bush administration's narrative of a dangerous Saddam Hussein in possession of dangerous weapons and in league with al Qaeda, they nonetheless suspected that some of these claims were overwrought. An advertisement in the *New York Times* paid for and signed by 33 respected academics concluded that the Bush administration had not presented conclusive evidence and that a war against Iraq lacked sufficient justification.

For the most part, they confined themselves to a narrower set of arguments—those pertaining to the harm that a costly and protracted war could inflict on U.S. national security. They disputed Pollack, Kristol, and Kaplan's claims that the war would end quickly. "Even if we win easily," they said, "we have no plausible exit strategy." The statement envisioned a long-term U.S. presence because Iraq was "a deeply divided society" and would take "many years to create a viable state." Lastly, the signatories of the *New York Times* advertisement saw the war in Iraq as a dangerous distraction from the more urgent concern: al Qaeda and transnational terrorism. "Al Qaeda poses a greater threat to the U.S. than does Iraq. War with Iraq will jeopardize the campaign against al Qaeda by diverting resources and attention from that campaign and by increasing anti-Americanism around the globe."[18]

Two of the organizers and signatories of the *Times* advertisement, the University of Chicago's John Mearsheimer and Harvard's Stephen Walt, followed up with an essay in *Foreign Policy* magazine, based on an earlier academic paper. They challenged the implicit assumption behind the case for war, namely that Hussein could not be deterred from using the weapons that many assumed he had. Because they believed Hussein had been, and would continue to be, deterred from acting against those who could retaliate against him, they argued that it would be a mistake for the United States to initiate a preventive war. "Even if such a war goes well and has positive long-range consequences, it will still have been unnecessary," Mearsheimer and Walt wrote. "And if it goes badly—whether in the form of high U.S. casualties, significant civilian deaths, a heightened risk of terrorism, or increased hatred of the United States in the Arab and Islamic world—then its architects will have even more to answer for."[19]

Within the Beltway, most foreign policy experts either endorsed Bush's war or kept their silence. Scholars at the Cato Institute, however, were particularly active in their opposition. Cato chairman William Niskanen came forward with one of the earliest arguments against war with Iraq, in December 2001, in a debate at the institute with former CIA director James Woolsey, and in a follow-up article in the *Chicago Sun-Times* under the headline "U.S. Should Refrain from Attacking Iraq."[20] "An unnecessary war," Niskanen observed, "is an unjust war."[21]

Other Cato scholars joined in. Ted Galen Carpenter, vice president for defense and foreign policy studies at the time, challenged the war boosters' optimistic predictions of a short and cheap engagement. "The inevitable U.S. military victory," Carpenter predicted, would "mark the start of a new round of headaches. Ousting Saddam would make Washington responsible for Iraq's political future and entangle the United States in an endless nation-building mission beset by intractable problems."[22] "Iraq [is] a fissiparous amalgam of Sunnis, separatist Shiites, and Kurds," noted Cato senior editor Gene Healy. "Keeping the country together will require a strong hand and threatens to make U.S. servicemen walking targets for discontented radicals."[23]

In December 2002, Cato published a comprehensive study making the case against war. Authors Ivan Eland and Bernard Gourley concluded:

> The United States deterred and contained a rival super-power, which had thousands of nuclear warheads, for 40 years; America can certainly continue to successfully deter and contain a relatively small, relatively poor nation until its leader dies or is deposed. An unprovoked attack on another sovereign state does not square with—and actually undermines—the principles of a constitutional republic.[24]

Such warnings failed to halt the march to war in Iraq, which killed more Americans than the 19 al Qaeda hijackers did on that horrible September day. Many hundreds of thousands of innocent men, women, and children have perished in both Iraq and Afghanistan. The Watson Institute of International and Public Affairs at Brown University estimated in November 2017 that the post-9/11 wars had cost the United States $5.6 trillion—more than three times higher than the Pentagon's own estimates at the time.[25]

But the so-called War on Terrorism entailed so much more. There are the undeclared wars, or the barely acknowledged wars, fought in dozens of places around the world. These include drone strikes on suspected terrorists from the air and raids by special operators on the ground. Those killed include U.S. citizens, denied their basic constitutional right to due process. Some of those who were captured alive were tortured, which is explicitly prohibited by both U.S. statute and international law. Supporters countered by euphemistically describing such methods as "enhanced interrogation techniques" and implying that the anti-torture laws did not apply. Other captives were subjected to "extraordinary rendition"—sent to secret prisons, often in dictatorships friendly to the United States, where in many cases they were tortured. Still others have languished for over 15 years in the U.S. facility in Guantanamo Bay, Cuba, trapped in a legal limbo between the customary laws of war and international and U.S. law.

Some of these acts have been sanctioned by legislation. In the days immediately after 9/11, Congress passed an Authorization for the Use of Military Force that granted the president wide latitude to go after those who perpetrated the 9/11 attacks and those who supported them. In the ensuing months, still more laws were passed, including the USA PATRIOT Act and legislation that created the Department of Homeland Security. But while the laws signaled Congress's willingness to go to great lengths to fight the terrorist menace, the post-9/11 era highlighted the steady erosion of Congress's power—a trend that first came into focus during the Great Depression and World War II and then accelerated during the Cold War. The clause of the Constitution that James Madison declared the most important of the entire document, that which vested the war powers with the Congress, not the White House, has been reduced to a nullity.[26] For the most part, U.S. presidents, possessing vast military capabilities, carry out attacks on their own authority. Oftentimes, the White House neglects to notify Congress at all, or only after the fact.

Such was the case when Barack Obama approved a mission to kill or capture Osama bin Laden. In 2011, the mastermind of the 9/11 attacks finally met his fate in Abbottabad, Pakistan, in a curious compound a short distance from the Kakul military academy, Pakistan's rough equivalent of West Point.[27]

Mission Accomplished

The documents recovered from the home where bin Laden had been hiding for six years revealed neither his grandiosity nor his genius. His dreams of creating a transnational caliphate were nothing more than the musings of a distant, disconnected figure with limited control over those who purportedly operated under his organization's banner. Nearly all the lone wolves and self-starters who attempted attacks after 9/11—from the failed shoe bomber Richard Reid, to the underwear bomber Umar Farouk Abdulmutallab, to the Times Square bomber Faisal Shahzad—managed to harm only themselves.

But in another sense, each of these would-be terrorists, and the man who inspired them all, succeeded in ways that they could have only imagined. Reid's failed attack convinced the Transportation Security Administration to require air travelers to remove their shoes during preflight screening procedures. Abdulmutallab's bomb didn't harm anyone other than himself. Fear that it might have, however, prompted the purchase and installation of thousands of full-body scanners at airports—dubbed a "virtual strip search" by critics.[28] Travelers who didn't want their private parts studied electronically could ask for a special screening (i.e., physical groping).

Osama bin Laden once bragged of being able to bleed the United States into bankruptcy. We seem well on our way toward both fiscal and moral bankruptcy. We have tolerated vast increases in spending to thwart would-be terrorists, and we have stuck our children and grandchildren with the bill. We have experienced a plethora of new laws and regulations designed to find terrorists or disrupt their plans. When those weren't enough, we have witnessed the U.S. government break the law and defy the Constitution. And we have waged war—many wars, actually—and yet the terrorism problem only seems to grow.

Terrorism works if its targets are terrorized. By that measure, the terrorists are winning. The land of the free and the home of the brave has willingly become the land of the prodded and surveilled and the home of the fearful.[29] When terrorists claiming allegiance to the so-called Islamic State, or ISIS, carried out a well-orchestrated attack in Paris in November 2015, U.S. politicians and pundits fell over themselves calling for draconian restrictions on immigrants, including women and children fleeing ISIS's savagery. Some claimed that the Paris attacks proved the need for even more intrusive surveillance of all Americans, most of whom, presumably, are innocent. Others pressed private firms to disable or hand over the keys to encryption technology that allows private citizens to evade government snooping. Still others contemplated creating a database to register all American Muslims. And President Donald Trump seems determined to discourage new Muslims from entering the country. Internment camps held Japanese Americans during World War II. Could the same unjust treatment befall Muslim Americans in the War on Terrorism? The possibility, dismissed as a reprehensible and repugnant proposition in the immediate aftermath of 9/11, seems all too plausible at the time of this writing.

All it would take, it seems, for Americans to willingly surrender more of their freedoms, more of their legal rights, more of their money, and more of their lives is another terrorist attack here in the United States.

Fear is the Health of the State

From a libertarian perspective, human history is a constant struggle to limit government and preserve individual liberty and autonomy. War and other crises have served as the primary vehicle for the growth of government. As noted in chapter 1, war is the health of the state. The American Founders knew this. Thus, they strived mightily to constrain the new government's powers to wage war. But in the end, the government's reach has expanded beyond anything that George Washington and his contemporaries could have imagined.

They anticipated, however, what was likely to upset their intricate plans for balancing the three branches against one another, for balancing the states against the federal government, and for balancing them all against the power of the people: fear.

Madison understood this dynamic well. Individual liberty is most at risk during periods of heightened anxiety. People are often willing to sacrifice some of their money or freedom or privacy in order to enhance their sense of security. It was "a universal truth," he wrote in a letter to Jefferson, "that the loss of liberty at home is to be charged to provision against danger, real or pretended from abroad."[30]

Others since then have stumbled upon similar ideas about how popular notions of threats—and fear of those threats—have been used to grow the power of government. "The whole aim of practical politics," opined the social critic and satirist H. L. Mencken, "is to keep the populace alarmed (and hence clamorous to be led to safety) by menacing it with an endless series of hobgoblins, most of them imaginary."[31]

Madison and Mencken's warnings remain relevant today. In November 2008, incoming Obama chief of staff Rahm Emanuel called for swift government action to deal with what he said was an urgent threat. "You never want a serious crisis to go to waste," Emanuel explained, as it's an "opportunity to do things you could not do before."[32]

While Emanuel was talking about an economic crisis, an increasingly powerful state can be used in many different ways, regardless of whether its growth was precipitated by fears of foreign threats or domestic ones. The same sorts of powers that allowed the Justice Department to go after suspected terrorists allowed the IRS to harass suspected Tea Partiers. Congress's abdication of its obligations under the Constitution and its acquiescence to the vast growth of executive power opens the door to further abuses when the next crisis hits.

* * *

So far, this book has documented the rise of the American state—especially the ways in which wars, and fears of war, have contributed to it. We have witnessed the vast growth of a national security bureaucracy and considered how and why that has occurred.

The book now turns to the principles and ideas that should inform our national security policies going forward. These alternatives are preferable to the status quo not merely because they would constrain the further growth of government and restore the balance between the citizen and the state, but because they are also more likely to advance our security and preserve our prosperity than the policies that have guided the United States' conduct in recent years.

Part II

The Elements of Modern Libertarian Foreign Policy

⑧

The Case for Skepticism

Your doctor might tell you that an ounce of prevention is worth a pound of cure, but there is a strong bias against preventive action in the realm of international affairs. While eating broccoli might be unappetizing, it won't kill you.

This bias is even stronger among libertarians than among non-libertarians, and it is informed by F. A. Hayek's teachings and writings. Libertarians are inclined against intervention in both foreign and domestic affairs because we doubt that such interventions will succeed at reasonable costs and fear the likely unintended consequences. This chapter will address these considerations.

The Fatal Conceit

Hayek was skeptical of government institutions. He advocated limited government, individual liberty, and market competition. He warned of the "fatal conceit," the presumption that "man is able to shape the world around him according to his wishes" without regard to the limits of his knowledge, and he warned of the unintended consequences that result from even the best-intentioned of human designs.[1] Although the Nobel laureate said relatively little about foreign policy in his long and distinguished career, his thoughts on government failure in domestic affairs retain their relevance when those governments turn their attentions abroad.

Human beings are hamstrung by the problem of imperfect and incomplete knowledge. Hayek showed how the government is incapable, over the long term, of managing the allocation of scarce goods and services. The government and its many agents cannot possibly know all that is needed to succeed. The signals that government receives are far inferior to those available in a marketplace through the price mechanism. Government officials rely instead on popular sentiment, as expressed (infrequently and incompletely) in elections or referendums. They consult with experts. And they also assess their own self-interest, presuming—not always correctly—that what is good for them will generally be good for the citizens they purport to serve.

Those who call for military action to overthrow an illiberal, undemocratic government in order to make way for a liberal, democratic one ignore the fatal conceit. So too do advocates for other types of preventive war.

Unlike preemption, in which a country acts in order to block an imminent hostile act, a preventive war is waged in anticipation of a threat that does not yet exist. Rather than waiting for that threat to materialize, advocates of preventive war call for acting now to forestall a worse outcome later.

One can see how this approach runs afoul of the knowledge problem.

Otto von Bismarck, the iconic statesman who created a unified Germany through a series of well-executed wars and diplomatic maneuvers, was highly skeptical of prevention. He never lost a war, but in his memoirs he pondered whether it might be "desirable, as regards a war which we should probably have to face sooner or later, to bring it on *anticipando* before the adversary could improve his preparations." Bismarck concluded that, generally speaking, it was not. "Even victorious wars cannot be justified unless they are forced upon" the statesman because he or she "cannot see the cards of Providence far enough ahead" to know that preventive action was justified.[2] The better course was to wait.

Consider how this works with respect to forcible regime change to install a democratic government in some foreign capital. How can we be certain that the existing undemocratic government will threaten us at some point in the future? After all, the United States has maintained peaceful relations with a number of undemocratic regimes, some for many years. The United States has had decent diplomatic relations with Morocco, a monarchy, for over two centuries.

We must not assume that a perfect government can or should be imposed at the barrel of a gun. Nor should we assume that regime change will necessarily produce a better government than the one that came before (see chapter 11). And we must also recognize that any attempt by an outside power to engineer a specific political outcome in any given place will often undermine or crowd out reformist elements within that country.

Even if it were possible to implant a new political order in states after we topple undemocratic governments there, that is not a sufficient pretext for military intervention. While we all look forward to the day when the world is populated by liberal, democratic nation-states committed to the rule of law, open markets, and respect for human rights (all things that libertarians value), it would be foolish to declare that any government that does not currently meet these standards is a candidate for overthrow. In short, even if war were easy and effective, we should still resist the impulse to initiate force.

This Time, It's Different: Rogue States, Terrorists, and WMDs

The case for prevention is made stronger, some might say, by the unique confluence of destructive capabilities and nihilistic ideologies. In an era of transnational terrorist groups such as al Qaeda or ISIS, and given the existence of mass-casualty weapons, we can't be absolutely certain—but merely reasonably confident—that a threat will materialize to which preventive action is a justified response.

But those inclined to buy into this logic must also account for government's propensity to fail. One could say that the preventive war model takes the old saying "if it ain't broke, don't fix it" and modifies it as follows: "If it ain't working just right and you're afraid that it might break in the future, then best break it now and then rebuild it so that it's working better than before."

The presumption under this model is that after we break a not-yet-completely-broken thing—for example, a country with an illegitimate, undemocratic government—what comes after will necessarily be an improvement.

But we must be confident that the new government is, in fact, a considerable improvement over that which came before, because we are talking about possibly spending hundreds of billions of dollars, threatening the destruction of property, and risking millions of lives. From a moral perspective, to say nothing of a prudential one, no one would argue that these risks would be justified by a modest improvement at the margin. Our merely replacing undemocratic tyrant A with undemocratic tyrant B would not warrant military intervention.

There are still some, however, who cling to their faith in intervention. They populate the halls of Congress, the executive branch, and the Washington institutions that serve as the holding pens for those out of office, waiting to go back in. Washington's interventionist bias—the nearly overwhelming impulse to do something, *anything*—has not been much tempered by the United States' experiences in Iraq and elsewhere in the Middle East, North Africa, and Central Asia.

The interventionist class was never enamored of Hayek's teachings. He told them what they couldn't do, why they would fail, and why the spontaneous order of the market was far superior to the rational-planning model favored by bureaucrats.

But the argument that preventive action and central planning can solve distant problems and reorder foreign societies to make them more friendly has taken a big hit in recent years.

One could argue that we didn't have sufficient evidence, especially in the immediate aftermath of the 9/11 terrorist attacks, to prove that Hayek was right. Perhaps we *could* achieve a decisive victory over foreign tyrants, as we appeared to have done in Afghanistan in late 2001? Perhaps the first Gulf War, in which U.S. forces drove Iraq's vaunted army from Kuwait in a matter of a few weeks, would be repeated in 2003? Maybe a little shock and awe, the reasoning went, would succeed again?

This seemed reasonable to many Americans at the time, although the evidence in late 2002 and early 2003—after the initial phases of operations in Afghanistan concluded—strongly suggested that toppling the Baathist regime in Iraq would be a lot harder than the advocates for war were claiming. The opponents of the war in Iraq failed to stop it. Fear, so endemic after 9/11, significantly reduced the public's willingness to tolerate brutal dictators in foreign lands who might—just might—ally themselves with terrorists. The fact that the United States remained closely allied with the dictatorship in Saudi Arabia generally escaped notice (see chapter 10).

The true costs of the Iraq war are now clear, and they reaffirm Hayek's warning about the fatal conceit. Many of the Iraqis who welcomed American troops as liberators, chiefly Shia Arabs and Kurds who had been so brutally oppressed by Saddam's government, turned against the United States when it was seen as blocking their hoped-for revenge. U.S. troops and U.S. government officials briefly tried to force Iraq's factions into a unity government that respected the rights of all Iraqis. It was hubris in the extreme. And the narrative of democracy promotion collapsed into farce when U.S. officials attempted to install into power their preferred Iraqis.

The U.S. military quickly began to look like the imperial armies of a bygone era, with U.S. officials as the potentates and viceroys. The United States would teach the Iraqis to elect good men—as Woodrow Wilson famously said he would do in Latin America—and create a functioning democracy in the heart of the Middle

East. This, in turn, would have a demonstration effect throughout the region.

It didn't work out that way. Iraqis began to see the U.S. troops not as liberators, but rather as occupiers. Attacks on U.S. forces rose. Foreign fighters flowed into Iraq to drive the Americans out. Al Qaeda, which didn't have a major presence in Iraq under Saddam Hussein, materialized there within a few years. Then, in 2014, fighters of the so-called Islamic State took advantage of the chaos and despair unleashed by the war to seize power across a wide swathe of Iraq and into Syria.

The experience of the Iraq war has not shaken the most fervent advocates of intervention. In 2015, for example, William Kristol asserted, simply, "We were right to invade Iraq in 2003."[3] Sen. Tom Cotton declared that "we should not be ashamed," after stating that "a leader has to . . . make a decision . . . based on the best information he has. George Bush did that in 2002 and 2003." Sen. Marco Rubio essentially agreed: "It was not a mistake for the president to go into Iraq."[4] In his book *The Big Stick*, Eliot Cohen of Johns Hopkins University's School of Advanced International Studies grudgingly allowed that "the Iraq war was a mistake,"[5] but in 2013 he concluded that "the basic rationale for the war [was] sound."[6] The notion that going to war in Iraq was the right thing to do, or that Iraq-like wars are justifiable, implies that we should be planning similar operations against similar despots. That such views persist despite the problems that we have encountered reveals the extent to which Hayek's warnings about the fatal conceit and the problem of knowledge have been discarded or ignored.

The Incompetence Dodge

The interventionists typically resort to criticizing the implementation and tactics instead of the original rationale for the war.[7] The problem, they say, is not that the Bush administration knocked off Hussein's government. The problem is that Bush administration officials were incompetent. They didn't use enough troops. They didn't secure the border. They disbanded the Iraqi army. They failed to provide water, power, and sanitation. They didn't provide security for disadvantaged groups. They didn't hand out enough money. They didn't hand out enough money quickly enough. Implicitly, those who still believe that war in Iraq was the right course of action in 2003 also believe that next time we'll get it right.

But why on earth would anyone believe that? Libertarians don't.

Such arguments echo those of government bureaucrats who when called to task for failing to educate kids or house the homeless or provide health care to the sick reply, "We need more." The problem was more complicated than we anticipated, they argue, but that doesn't mean we should stop trying to solve it. If we had more money, more people, more time, then we could get this right.

Hayek reminds us why such arguments are unconvincing. Just as military commanders know that battle plans never survive first contact with the enemy, so too do more ambitious plans collapse in the face of the messy realities of our complicated world. Central planning always falls short of expectations. Human beings cannot know—or reliably predict—the course of human events. If we could, the Soviet Union would have been a paradise for all.

If preventive action were merely foolish, we might dismiss it as harmless hubris.

But doing something for no good reason and to no good effect isn't merely a waste of resources. Because of the law of unintended consequences, preventive action may actually be worse than no action at all.[8]

Unintended Consequences

Hayek didn't only believe that government was likely to fail. He also believed that it was likely to make things worse.

It begins with unrealistic assumptions. It is rather like Sidney Harris's cartoon about the mathematician who develops an elaborate proof, written in longhand on a massive whiteboard. In the midst of a string of barely comprehensible symbols and numbers is written, "Then a miracle occurs."

One of his colleagues asks him to be more specific.

This message is particularly relevant whenever military action or other forms of coercive diplomacy are under consideration. It isn't enough for politicians and policymakers to tell us what actions they intend to take. It is also incumbent on them to explain, as precisely as possible, what they believe will happen as a result.

Put another way: show your work. How does the policy that you are advocating lead to the end that you seek?

Because international politics isn't subject to the iron laws of math or physics, a fair amount of speculation and supposition goes into policymaking. That is to be expected. We guess as to what might happen after a particular course of action is chosen, and our guesses are supported by reasonable expectations, the facts on the ground at that particular time, and past experience in similar or analogous situations.

But we must always be on guard. The facts are certainly subject to interpretation. The assumptions are even more speculative. Cause and effect are nearly inscrutable. Who is to say that *that* particular threat caused tyrant A to step down? Did the legislators in country Y vote to change a given policy as a direct result of economic pressure caused by international sanctions? Or did they decide that the policy had simply outlived its usefulness? In other words, would they likely have come to that same conclusion in the absence of foreign pressure?

Meanwhile, history isn't necessarily useful here, and it rarely produces a definitive answer. Reasoning by analogy is a perilous enterprise. No two cases are identical. What worked before may not work again, and contingency rules the day. Invoking a particular historical case to prove the wisdom or folly of acting in the present is as likely to lead to misinterpretation and misjudgment as it is to produce an obvious solution to a vexing problem.

In his book *Myths of Empire*, Columbia University's Jack Snyder discusses a particular type of misconception that is often compounded by misreading history. He calls it the "paper tiger" thesis. On the one hand, a foreign threat is deemed serious enough that preventive action is warranted to eliminate it. On the other hand, the capabilities of the adversary in question are minimal, and it would easily be vanquished after a short and decisive war. Hawks cite past instances of short and decisive wars to make the case for the use of force. Cases that do not conform to the paper tiger thesis—for example, when a threatened adversary chooses to fight rather than tuck tail and run away—are dismissed as inapplicable. While the risks of inaction are always portrayed as very high, the risks of action are cast as negligible. Snyder shows why it is generally unwise to base a country's foreign policy on the best case, the paper tiger thesis. It is, as the title of his book suggests, one of the myths of empire. Hayek would call it part and parcel of the fatal conceit.[9]

The Precautionary Principle

A similar mindset explains modern governments' approach to the introduction of new products, foods, or medicines. The precautionary principle holds that whenever something might pose a threat to human life or public health, the government should take preventive (precautionary) action to mitigate that possible harm, even if the scientific evidence is incomplete or the costs of such preventive action are very high. The burden of proof for demonstrating that something is *not* harmful falls on those wishing to introduce a new product or initiate some new action. In the meantime, government intervention is warranted.

University of Chicago law professor Cass Sunstein observes that the precautionary principle, in practice, often entails a substantial misallocation of resources.[10] Any action taken to deal with a given threat necessarily involves dedicating fewer resources to some other danger. Meanwhile, the law of unintended consequences dictates that any one government action to deal with a given set of problems is likely to generate a host of new issues. At a minimum, any given intervention should attempt to capture both the costs and risks of action against the costs and risks of inaction. Former Cato research fellow Benjamin H. Friedman explains that this "does not mean that states should not regulate against uncertain dangers" but rather that such "dangers should be evaluated by cost-benefit analysis." This would include assessing "the cost that preventive action would avert, the likelihood that preventive action will work, and the action's cost."[11] Typically, however, such judgements rely on speculation about the magnitude and likelihood of the possible harm. Adjudicating these disputes is a matter of politics, not probability or mathematics. Those most motivated to prevent the possible danger are inclined to play up the risks; those wishing to avoid the imposition of regulations stress the high costs of prevention and downplay the likelihood of harm in the absence of proactive government intervention.

A particular form of the precautionary principle applies to national security policy. Without the typical push and pull of competing parties making arguments for or against intervention, uncertainty itself becomes a danger worth defending against. But the "unique attributes of security dangers do not remove the danger of precautionary reasoning," Friedman explains:

> True, uncertain dangers of potentially great and irreversible consequence merit extensive preventive efforts. That is why states have traditionally devoted large portions of their budgets to defense. But high uncertainty and potential consequences do not mean that states can ignore the costs of defenses. Moreover, national security dangers are not always as uncertain and dangerous as we hear.[12]

Vice President Dick Cheney's 1 percent doctrine from the early days of the Global War on Terror represents a particularly extreme form of precautionary thinking, which had similarly extreme effects. As reported by author Ron Suskind, Cheney believed that "if there was even a 1 percent chance of terrorists getting a weapon of mass destruction—and there has been a small probability of such an occurrence for some time—the United States must now act as if it were a certainty."[13]

Friedman succinctly explains the problem with such reasoning. While it is appropriate for states to take action to prevent an unlikely but catastrophic event, he writes:

> [P]retending that the catastrophe is certain justifies overly risky and expensive preventive action. If there is a one percent chance of a $10,000 problem, you should not want to pay insurance worth more than $100 to prevent it. If the odds are certain, you'll pay anything less than $10,000. That is the kind of reasoning that makes a $600 billion defense budget and the Iraq war seem sensible.[14]

Friedman demonstrates the dangers of exaggerating risks and downplaying costs when it comes to national security policy. He concludes: "No formula tells us how to maximize safety. But skepticism—toward both what we are told to fear and the defenses we are sold to confront it—is a good start."[15]

We shouldn't suspend our disbelief when advocates of intervention claim that it will deliver the hoped-for end. We should be particularly wary of allegedly minor interventions that threaten to grow into wider conflicts. Not every brush-fire war will turn into a full-scale conflagration between major states, but in the nuclear era we should be particularly on guard against possible unintended consequences. We must choose our battles wisely.

Alas, current U.S. grand strategy—"primacy"—advises against picking and choosing. We turn to the flaws of this strategy in the next chapter.

9

The Problem with American Primacy

A suicide bombing in Yemen kills scores of new military recruits. Zimbabwe's president Robert Mugabe is deposed in a palace coup. Nuclear-armed North Korea tests ballistic missiles. Venezuela is in a political and economic death spiral. Syria's civil war drags on with no end in sight. In each case, a worried world asks: "What is the United States going to do?"[1]

U.S. policymakers have invited this response. For decades, Washington has pursued a quixotic goal of primacy, also known as "deep engagement" or "global hegemony." It presumes that the United States is the world's "indispensable nation."[2] That means that U.S. leadership is required in order to solve every problem, in any part of the world. All of these problems will grow worse if the United States fails to act, according to this logic. "We stand tall and we see further than other countries into the future," Secretary of State Madeleine Albright explained in 1998, "and we see the danger here to all of us."[3]

This belief in Washington's supposed twin powers of perfect prognostication and always-effective action persists despite the unpleasant reality that policymakers have often guessed wrong or have failed even when they correctly identified the problem. U.S. policymakers' commitment to maintaining preponderant military power, not merely to defend the United States but also to defend a growing roster of security dependents, has likewise proved surprisingly resilient, even as the relative difficulty of maintaining this posture has grown. That is unfortunate for a number of reasons, including the high costs and dubious benefits, but mostly because the core assumptions underlying U.S. foreign policy are deeply flawed and deserve a full public airing.

That foreign policy status quo, primacy, hinges on the belief that overwhelming American power makes the world safer—and not merely our possession of great power, but our willingness to use it. The U.S. military exists to defend this country and its vital security interests, but—critically—it also defends others. Primacy holds that it would be too dangerous to allow other countries to defend themselves. Some will fail, necessitating U.S. interventions at a later date under less auspicious circumstances. Others will succeed too well, unleashing arms races that could roil regions or even the whole planet. Primacists are particularly concerned about self-help leading to nuclear proliferation. If countries were driven out from under the security umbrella provided by American nuclear weapons, the argument goes, then some—perhaps many—would seek a nuclear arsenal of their own.[4]

Thus, one could say that the greatest fear among U.S. leaders since the end of World War II has been other countries' fears.

U.S. foreign policy aims to reassure a nervous world. Primacy calls on the U.S. military to stop threats from materializing: threats anywhere, to almost anyone (or at least the United States' 60-plus formal and de facto treaty allies). And when prevention fails and fires ignite, the United States is the first on the scene to stomp them out.

Writing in 1993, the dawn of the post–Cold War era, Harvard political scientist Samuel Huntington contended that "a world without U.S. primacy will be a world with more violence and disorder and less democracy and economic growth."[5] A quarter century later, most U.S. foreign policy experts agree that U.S. primacy is essential to global peace and prosperity and is the key factor in the spread of democracy, liberalism, and human rights. The U.S. global cop, explains the *New York Times*'s Bret Stephens, must continue to walk the "old beat, a reassuring presence in a still-dangerous world."[6]

Primacy in such a big world requires the world's largest, most powerful, and most expensive military—and the U.S. military is all those things. Notwithstanding mostly Republican claims that Barack Obama "gutted" the U.S. military, the facts show otherwise. Defense spending in the eight years under Barack Obama exceeded that under George W. Bush, and by a wide margin. After adjusting for inflation, the annual average from 2009 to 2016 was nearly 17 percent higher than that from 2001 to 2008.

Yet despite such increases in U.S. military spending over the past two decades, policymakers worry that the U.S. military is unprepared to fulfill its missions. In other words, the costs merely to maintain the status quo are growing more onerous, not less. So long as primacy reigns supreme, these costs will fall almost entirely on the backs of U.S. taxpayers, while the risks will be borne almost exclusively by U.S. soldiers, sailors, airmen, and marines.

But the high cost of primacy is not its greatest shortcoming. The United States *could* spend more on its military, if it were truly essential. The real problem with primacy is that it isn't necessary to maintain U.S. security. Instead, it undermines it by increasing the likelihood that the United States will become drawn into other people's fights. And once involved, the United States becomes responsible for bringing those fights to an acceptable conclusion—or it's blamed for failing to do so.

Consider just three of primacy's key assumptions: 1) that technology has rendered geography moot, subjecting the United States to more threats, and more urgent ones, than ever before; 2) that primacy is essential to the health of the international economy; and 3) that discouraging allies—even stable democracies—from maintaining military power contributes to global peace and stability. None of these assumptions holds. This chapter scrutinizes the first two of these beliefs, while the subsequent chapter considers the issue of alliances under primacy.

Our (Not So) Dangerous World

For the first 100 years or so of American history, U.S. leaders relied on what the University of Chicago's John Mearsheimer calls "the stopping power of water"[8] as the country's principal means of defense. Washington urged his countrymen to take advantage of "our detached and distant station" and maintain a neutral stance with respect to other nations.[9]

It didn't always work—think Washington, DC, set ablaze during the War of 1812 when the U.S. Navy was weak and the British Navy was strong—but that was the exception that proves the rule. This is particularly true in the modern era, when the United States enjoys overwhelming military superiority, including a prodigious nuclear deterrent. Indeed, the United States enjoys what Eric Nordlinger over 20 years ago called "strategic immunity."[10]

Are things really so different today? Has technology evaporated the seas, allowing large land armies to march across the ocean floor? Is the world now a single global village?

No, explains Patrick Porter, author of *The Global Village Myth.* "Technology may accelerate movement," but "it does not necessarily shrink strategic space," enabling countries to easily project power. In fact, Porter writes, "projecting power affordably over space is now more difficult, not less." This reality constrains both superpowers and their adversaries, making "us all less powerful, but more secure, than we think."[11] Certain technologies can make water barriers, for example, even more formidable than in the past. Low-cost and nearly ubiquitous surveillance is available even to nonstate actors. Precision-guided missiles and smart mines can target even the most sophisticated modern warships, turning even narrow bodies of water into no-go zones, or what Notre Dame's Eugene Gholz calls "no-man's seas."[12]

Land invasions, meanwhile, are made much more costly by economic interdependence and the presence of nuclear weapons. Russia's Vladimir Putin seized territory in two neighboring states—Georgia in 2008 and Ukraine in 2014—but relied on mysterious "little green men" in eastern Ukraine, partly out of fear of the international reaction. The Baltic states on Russia's border—Estonia and Latvia—are covered under NATO's nuclear umbrella. Outright aggression against either of these small countries, along the lines even of what was attempted in Georgia and Ukraine, would almost surely elicit an overwhelming response. But Russia, or any other foreign invader, must also contend with nationalist resistance. The diffusion of new technologies has made it easier for the poor-but-determined to challenge much stronger and richer global actors.[13]

This is also true in Asia, where Beijing has converted a share of China's rising economic power into a formidable military. It will be hard, however, for Beijing to project power by sea, even against nearby islands like Taiwan. China's audacious bid to become one of the very few countries in the world to operate even a single (small) aircraft carrier won't solve the problem of distance. Meanwhile, it does have more urgent problems. As China's economic growth slows down and the risk of popular unrest rises, the People's Liberation Army is likely to focus on maintaining domestic order at home, not upsetting it abroad.

What of other types of threats, besides land invasion and occupation by foreign armies? Surely these merit greater attention, the primacists would say. We cannot rely on oceans to halt nuclear missiles that fly over them or to prevent cyberattacks in the ethereal realm. And terrorists could infiltrate by land, sea, or air—or be grown right here at home.

But our own nuclear weapons are a powerful deterrent against state actors with return addresses, and primacy is all but irrelevant when dealing with terrorists and hackers. Timely intelligence is almost always more helpful than warships or fighter planes for law enforcement agencies trying to roll up criminal gangs. The use of deadly force may be appropriate—to thwart an imminent attack, for example—but such operations should be combined with non-kinetic measures that advance a broader agenda and drain away support from terrorists or nonstate actors. Well-intentioned and carefully planned military strikes that nevertheless result in civilian casualties and collateral damage often have the opposite effect.

There have always been dangers in the world, and there always will be. To the extent that we can identify myriad threats that our ancestors couldn't fathom, primacy compounds the problem. By calling on the United States to deal with all threats, to all people, in all places, primacy ensures that even distant problems become our own.

Primacy Doesn't Pay

Primacists view the world differently. They argue that the United States must maintain a global military presence to protect the world economy. Some go so far as to argue that U.S. military power is *essential* to the proper functioning of the international economic system. The United States sets the rules of the game and punishes those who defy them. And by discouraging security competition among states, primacy creates the conditions for global trade. "U.S. security commitments help maintain an open world economy," write Stephen G. Brooks, G. John Ikenberry, and William C. Wohlforth.[14] If the United States were less inclined to intervene in other people's disputes, the primacists say, the risk of war would grow, roiling skittish markets. According to Edwin

Feulner, Arthur Brooks, and William Kristol, "Global prosperity requires commerce and trade, and this requires peace." They also challenged those who believed that America's fiscal crisis compelled it to revisit its military spending: "A weaker, cheaper military will not solve our financial woes. It will, however, make the world a more dangerous place, and it will impoverish our future."[15]

These are not new ideas. Economic historian Charles Kindleberger first popularized hegemonic stability theory, and it has become something of a religion among many U.S. foreign policy elites.[16]

Hegemonic stability theorists also claim that the U.S. military's global policing mission gives Americans leverage in economic negotiations with others, allowing us to shape the rules to advantage U.S. producers and consumers. To be sure, everyone gains—but the hegemon gains the most. A 2005 study by the Peterson Institute for International Economics estimated that the post-1945 global trading order adds $1 trillion to the U.S. economy every year.[17]

But the supposed economic benefits of U.S. military hegemony do not offset the costs. Political scientist Daniel Drezner finds that although America's massive military power "plays a supporting role," it does not by itself confer great benefits for the American economy. What's more, those benefits are diminishing over time. "The principal benefits that come with military primacy," Drezner writes, "appear to flow only when coupled with economic primacy." "An excessive reliance on military power, to the exclusion of other dimensions of power," he concludes, "will yield negative returns."[18]

University of Notre Dame professor and Cato adjunct scholar Eugene Gholz is even more emphatic that attempting to keep the peace on a global basis doesn't pay. Building on earlier work with Dartmouth's Daryl G. Press challenging the claims that foreign conflicts impose grave harm on neutral nations' economies, Gholz shows that "military instability overseas does not generally present a threat to the United States, unless the United States joins the fight." "The bottom line," Gholz concludes,

> is that it is rarely, if ever, worth spending American resources to prevent foreign instability in the hope of protecting American prosperity, even assuming that such spending effectively tamps down tension. The threat of economic damage, like many other threats, is often exaggerated.[19]

Primacists similarly overstate the role that the U.S. military plays in facilitating global trade, and they ignore the extent to which U.S. military activism has roiled markets and upset vital regions. At best, American military dominance is a double-edged sword, and a costly one at that.

For example, primacists claim that American military dominance confers unique economic benefits. As the dominant player, rule-maker, and the de facto enforcer of global norms, the United States after World War II was able to coerce weaker players into following its lead. On several occasions, Washington threatened and cajoled alliance partners to accede to its demands, particularly as it applied to sustaining the United States' capacity for spending well beyond its means. U.S. allies acted to shore up the dollar on a number of occasions when inflation worries mounted. But U.S. policymakers were compelled to act as well, explains historian Francis Gavin, often "sacrificing economic for geopolitical interests," particularly during the early Cold War.[20]

Not everyone agrees with this assessment, but many would concede that conditions have changed; after the fall of the Soviet Union, fewer security clients were willing to defer to Washington on matters of trade and economic policy. The nature of the threat had changed, and the ever-evolving international economic order offered them practical alternatives to the dollar-dominated system of the 1950s, 60s, and 70s. The 2008 financial crisis delivered a second major blow to the United States' authority. As U.S. military and, especially, economic dominance wanes relative to other international actors, America's ability to act as both "system maker and privilege taker" will further diminish.[21]

Even if that were not the case, we should question the suggestion that both U.S. companies' ability to sell in foreign markets and American consumers' taste for things produced outside of the United States would evaporate in the absence of U.S. military dominance. "It is not American troops deployed overseas that make American products and services attractive to foreign consumers," note Eugene Gholz, Daryl G. Press, and Harvey M. Sapolsky in a seminal critique of primacy, "it is the quality of American goods, the image of America's prosperity, and the productivity of American workers."[22]

Primacists assert that countries are more inclined to cut trade deals with the United States if the U.S. military protects them. It isn't obvious, however, that such negotiations are much influenced by the nature of the security relationships between trading partners; many countries would want to do business with some of the wealthiest consumers on the planet even if U.S. policymakers didn't promise to protect the sellers. Meanwhile, it is hard to extract concessions from security clients because U.S. threats to leave alliances are not credible. As a practical matter, then, write Benjamin H. Friedman, Brendan Rittenhouse Green, and Justin Logan, primacy entails "paying . . . allies for the privilege of defending them."[23]

In short, primacy hinges on a faith in the efficacy of U.S. military power that defies logic and willfully ignores recent history. It exaggerates the dangers facing the United States, in part because it takes on everyone's vulnerabilities as if they were our own. Primacy counts dubious economic benefits as certain assets and understates or ignores the mounting costs. It imagines a frail and brittle economic order prone to frequent disruptions and with too few parties invested in sustaining it. On the contrary, notes Columbia's Robert Jervis, "the developed countries have relatively little to gain by exploiting each other, and much to lose if cooperation breaks down."[24]

Policymakers should therefore be open to alternatives. One of the reasons so many resist change, however, is because of its impact on U.S. allies. We turn to the unique set of problems posed by permanent alliances in the next chapter.

10

Free Riders, Reckless Drivers, and Perilous Partners

In his Farewell Address, George Washington bequeathed to his fellow citizens a set of foreign policy principles that he hoped would endure long after he departed public life. The United States, he said, should strive for equality and impartiality with foreign nations, even in its commercial relations, "neither seeking nor granting exclusive favors or preferences." He urged his successors to establish the best rules governing trade and diplomacy "that present circumstances and mutual opinion will permit, but temporary, and liable to be from time to time abandoned or varied, as experience and circumstances shall dictate."

But above all else, Washington spoke at length about the dangers of foreign influence and of allowing U.S. policy to become too closely aligned with that of any other country: "It is folly in one nation to look for disinterested favors from another. . . . There can be no greater error than to expect or calculate upon real favors from nation to nation. It is an illusion, which experience must cure, which a just pride ought to discard."[1]

This pattern of avoiding permanent alliances and adjusting U.S. foreign policies on a case-by-case basis held for nearly 150 years. But, beginning in earnest in World War II, the United States formally allied itself with a host of nations, retained many of these alliances after the war, and then expanded its alliances during and after the Cold War. Today, for many experts, preserving U.S. alliances has become the *object* of U.S. foreign policy—not merely a means for advancing U.S. security. In 2012, then–Secretary of State Hillary Clinton explained that global leadership defined "who we are as Americans. It truly is in our DNA. And that's what makes us such an exceptional country."[2]

As discussed in the previous chapter, the dominant foreign policy paradigm, primacy, holds that it would be too dangerous to allow other countries to defend themselves and their interests. Some will botch the job, react too slowly, and fail to halt aggressors in a timely fashion, necessitating costly U.S. intervention later. The experience prior to World War II informs this point of view.

In other respects, however, primacy aims to discourage countries from taking steps to defend themselves. It hinges on the belief that countries will try too hard and succeed too well. The key event here is World War I, when arms races between the major powers contributed to international tensions and eventually a devastating conflict. Rather than relying on a loose collection of shifting treaties and alliances to maintain order, the United States holds itself out as *the* alliance partner for more than 60 countries around the world. U.S. foreign policy, therefore, is aimed at convincing these alliance partners that such arms buildups are unnecessary.

Indeed, reassurance is one of the central organizing principles of U.S. foreign policy, and therefore military force planning, today.

Consider, for example, the following sampling of headlines from major news outlets during a typical three-month period in the summer of 2017:

- "U.S. Reassures Australia of Continued Close Ties," Associated Press, June 5, 2017
- "U.S. Troops Reassure Allies in Poland Ahead of Trump's G-20 Visit," NBC News, July 5, 2017
- "Pence Travels to Baltic States to Reassure Allies and Send Message to Russia," *Washington Post*, July 30, 2017
- "Pentagon's Mattis Again Seeks to Reassure U.S. Allies," Reuters, August 19, 2017

There are, however, a number of problems with this approach. First of all, while U.S. guarantees of security to wealthy allies may have discouraged harmful arms races that might eventually have led to offensive wars, they have also caused those allies to underprovide for their own defense. This means that they have little capacity for dealing with common security challenges, from ethnic violence in the Balkans in the 1990s, to combatting terrorism and piracy in South Asia or the Horn of Africa in the 2000s, to averting state collapse in North Africa and the Middle East and the rise of the so-called Islamic State in the 2010s.

This underprovision of collective security goods was both predictable and predicted.[3] When the economists Mancur Olson and

Richard Zeckhauser first considered public goods theory in an international context, they observed that such goods were quite rare and would not operate in the same way as public goods in a strictly domestic sphere.[4] Scholars and U.S. public officials routinely hold up U.S. power as the stereotypical example of a global public good. But the problem is that it is neither a global good nor a public good.

Public goods, by definition, have two key characteristics. First, once provided, their benefits cannot be easily denied to those for whom they were not intended. Economists call this the principle of nonexcludability. The second key feature of public goods is that the value of the good is not diminished as additional consumers partake of it. This is known as nonrivalrous consumption.

Olson suggests a hypothetical parade down a city street to demonstrate how this works.[5] First of all, the good must be defined by the particular customers that it is intended to serve. For the individuals who purchase tickets to sit along the parade route, the spectacle is a private good not so different from any other form of entertainment, from concerts to sporting events. But for the people living in tall buildings that overlook the streets along which the parade passes, it is a free good. They have not paid to watch it, but it would be impractical to try to exclude them. The organizers, therefore, expect some degree of free riding. And the experience is the same whether 100 people watch the parade or 100,000 do. It is thus nonrivalrous.

Now consider the difference between that hypothetical example in a domestic context and an actual collective security alliance. Because the alliance's combined assets are not infinite, the allocation of some of them to defend one ally necessarily diminishes the amount available to defend others. A single brigade deployed to deter an attack on Estonia cannot simultaneously have the same deterrent effect in Romania. The security good is thus, obviously, not nonrivalrous.

Nor is it nonexcludable. Someone must decide how to allocate these scarce resources, and they can and should do so according to some criteria. Some alliance members will be able to enjoy the benefit; others will not. Some allies will be effectively excluded. And non-allies will be as well. Benefits provided can also be denied.

If challenged, defenders of the status quo might admit that U.S. foreign policy isn't a public good in the textbook sense; rather, the United States' various efforts on behalf of others, explains Michael Mandelbaum, amount to "gifts because these countries neither request nor pay for them." Americans provide these gifts because the costs of doing so are supposedly small and incidental to actions that we undertake mostly for our benefit. Mandelbaum likens the situation to that of a wealthy person who pays security guards to protect his property from miscreants. "Their presence," he writes, "will serve to protect the neighboring houses as well, even though their owners contribute nothing to the cost of the guards."[6]

But the merits of the current system, whereby the average American "pays and the rest of the world . . . benefits without having to pay,"[7] are more dubious than they might seem at first glance. For one thing, the analogy of a neighborhood watch falls apart when one considers that a majority of U.S. allies are not, except in the loosest possible sense of the word, in America's neighborhood.

Nor is it clear that the neighborhood is generally safer when one homeowner pays and the rest free-ride. After all, no one benefits if the occupants of the other houses discontinue their home monitoring systems, leave their doors and cars unlocked, and advertise the fact for all to see. This tendency of the weaker members of a security alliance to free-ride on the strong and grow still weaker in the process is endemic. And it cannot be easily reversed by a concerted campaign to shame the free riders into paying their fair share; individuals are generally disinclined to pay for things that others are willing to buy for them, and our threats to cut off our alliance partners for failing to share the burdens are generally not believed, because they are not true. The United States has never cut off an ally for failure to pay. The result is many allies with liabilities and very few with capabilities.

A second problem with U.S. alliances is that they are structured on the presumption of impartiality, a presumption that is neither believable nor believed. It rests, explains Francis Fukuyama, on a notion of "American exceptionalism that most non-Americans simply find not credible."[8]

The suggestion that the United States evenhandedly performs the role of world policeman defies common sense. Consider the analogy of a police officer tasked with patrolling a few city blocks. If his mother or grandmother lived on one of those blocks, it wouldn't surprise anyone if he spent more time there than on the rest of his beat. But while understandable, it would not be appropriate. It is a classic case of conflict of interest. The solution to the problem is to assign the cop to a part of the city where he did not have any particular personal connection. This is because the impulse to allow one's personal feelings and obligations to override a public duty is quite strong, and it would be unfair to the other prospective beneficiaries of his police work if he afforded them relatively less attention.

As Fukuyama observes, "The idea that the United States behaves disinterestedly on the world stage is not widely believed because it is for the most part not true and, indeed, could not be true if American leaders fulfill their responsibilities to the American people."[9] Citizens expect leaders to serve their interests. And any constituency most certainly would object if its own government, in serving others, provided a disservice to it.

The U.S. foreign policy elites' strong desire to mask the self-interested aspects of U.S. foreign policy leads them into a third set of problems: the American people, believing that U.S. foreign policy should first and foremost advance U.S. security interests, do not support one that is focused chiefly on the security interests of distant states or peoples.

"Americans approach the world much as other people do," Michael Mandelbaum grudgingly admitted. "For the American public, foreign policy, like charity, begins at home."[10] For that reason above all others, Mandelbaum predicted that "the American role in the world may depend in part on Americans not scrutinizing it too closely."[11]

When Americans do begin to ask questions, policymakers resort to misdirection and subterfuge. They push, prod, and occasionally even hoodwink Americans into taking on unnecessary tasks.

This manifests itself in two major ways: threat exaggeration or professions of beneficence.

In the first instance, U.S. leaders hype the threat—a practice that has gone on for decades. Recall, for example, the discussion of the early Cold War period when Harry Truman spoke "clearer than truth" to "scare the hell out of the American people." But this was hardly an isolated incident. Information asymmetries consistently work on behalf of the threat inflators. The explosion onboard the USS *Maine* in Havana Harbor in 1898 gave rise to the rallying cry "Remember the *Maine*" in the Spanish–American War. A curious episode involving U.S. naval vessels in the Gulf of Tonkin off the coast of Vietnam in 1964 paved the way for President Lyndon Johnson's massive expansion of an officially undeclared war. To build the case for war with Iraq, Vice President Dick Cheney warned of furtive meetings between 9/11 hijacker Mohammed Atta and Iraqi intelligence agents, and Secretary of State Colin Powell alleged that Saddam Hussein had a well-concealed chemical- and biological-weapons program.

The details about all of these incidents emerged long after the wars they respectively triggered had come and gone. Two different investigations by the U.S. Navy failed to prove Spain's complicity in the destruction of the *Maine*; some have speculated that spontaneous combustion in a coal storage bunker set off ammunition in a neighboring magazine.[12] The incident that deepened U.S. involvement in Vietnam was equally suspicious. Within hours of the report that North Vietnamese PT boats had fired torpedoes against two U.S. Navy destroyers, the *Maddox* and *Turner Joy*, the senior naval officer on the scene cabled a warning back to Washington: "Review of action makes many reported contacts and torpedoes fired appear doubtful. Freak weather effects on radar and overeager sonarmen may have accounted for many reports."[13] And as for Saddam Hussein's purported weapons program and ties to al Qaeda, a Senate inquiry in 2008 concluded that Bush administration officials had exaggerated the available intelligence and ignored dissenting views within the government in order to build the case for war.[14] We can expect similar murky incidents to serve as the rationale for attacks on any number of other modern-day boogeymen, from Iran's mad mullahs to North Korea's crazy Kims.

In the second instance, rather than appeal to fear, war advocates sting the collective conscience of the American people. However, the more that U.S. foreign policy succeeds as advertised and that our professions of solidarity are believed by the allies we claim to be protecting, the more those very facts will undermine support for intervention among the people who actually pay for such policies: American taxpayers and U.S. troops. Polling data often show that protecting U.S. allies is near the bottom of a list of Americans' foreign policy priorities, though that has started to shift in recent years.[15]

If nothing else, the persistence of America's alliances reflects a profound inability to adapt to changing circumstances. At times, however, it reveals confirmation bias: believing that the Soviet Union was bent on global domination, we interpreted Moscow's every action as a move in that direction. Still, extending U.S. security guarantees to the countries of Western Europe and East Asia after World War II made sense. The nations of Europe and East Asia were physically broken and fiscally broke, and we wanted to prevent the emergence of Japan and Germany as rivals. U.S.

officials continued to protect these countries during the entirety of the Cold War. If the United States had withdrawn from Asia and Europe, the thinking went, that could have left an imbalance of power that the Red Army or Communist China might have exploited. We now know that intelligence assessments, from the late Cold War period in particular, regularly inflated Moscow's capacity and appetite for all-out war.

But while the world changed after 1989, U.S. foreign policy largely did not. Indeed, the United States invited many new countries to join NATO, dramatically expanding the number of de facto permanent U.S. allies. A strategy document prepared by officials in the George H. W. Bush administration explained that the object of U.S. foreign policy in the post–Cold War era was to "prevent the re-emergence of a new rival" capable of challenging U.S. power in any vital region. The United States would retain preponderant military power, the Defense Planning Guidance explained, not merely to deter attacks against the United States but also to deter "potential competitors"—including long-time allies such as Germany and Japan—"from even aspiring to a larger regional or global role."[16]

One could say, in retrospect, that this strategy worked too well; Germany and Japan have often neglected to address security challenges in their respective regions. On the other hand, the strategy has not succeeded in preventing rivals from challenging U.S. power, and it has been extremely costly for U.S. troops and taxpayers.

There is nothing wrong with alliances, per se. As George Washington observed, countries have often banded together to address common security challenges. But permanent alliances are another matter entirely, and permanent alliances that fail to adapt to changing circumstances are the worst sort of all. Under the current arrangement, we agree to defend our wealthy allies and they agree to let us. That creates an unnecessarily fragile system whereby the American peoples' willingness to wage war on others' behalf becomes a single point of failure. If Americans withhold their support for a particular distant mission, then the rest of the world—trapped by its dependence on U.S. power—is practically paralyzed by its limited capabilities.

Primacy discourages others from acting to address urgent nearby threats before they become regional or global crises. Though informed by reasonable concerns about security dilemmas and arms races, this approach has gone too far. We need more capable and willing actors in the world. A more resilient approach would therefore ask more of our allies and security partners today and in the future. We shouldn't expect them only to cheer us on from the sidelines when we act militarily abroad. We shouldn't demand that they allow us to merely use our facilities in their lands. Rather, we should anticipate that they will act first. In short, we should expect—and in many cases demand—that other countries take primary responsibility for protecting their security and preserving their interests. Restraining our impulse to wage war when our vital national interests are not threatened would contribute to a more durable international system, one that was not overly dependent upon the U.S. military and the American people's willingness to use that military.

Perilous Partners

Reassured allies may be less inclined to take actions that threaten their neighbors. U.S. pledges to protect others from danger reduce the possibility of harmful and destabilizing arms races. Some measure of free riding and cheap riding, in other words, is an intended byproduct of U.S. foreign policy. "America is better served," explains *New York Times* columnist Bret Stephens, "by a world of supposed freeloaders than by a world of foreign policy freelancers."[17]

But reassurance can contribute to a different form of freelancing: with free riding and cheap riding, notes MIT's Barry Posen, comes "reckless driving."[18] Reassured allies might be less inclined to capitulate to powerful adversaries, but they might also refuse reasonable concessions that would preserve the peace. In some cases, they might be emboldened to undertake risky military operations, confident that Uncle Sam has their backs.

Take, for example, the countries of the Middle East. The United States has had a near permanent presence in the region for decades, but the region has also been torn by repeated wars, many of them started—or at least accelerated—by U.S. allies.

Heavy diplomatic U.S. involvement in the Middle East goes back at least to the end of World War II. In the waning days of the war in February 1945, President Franklin Delano Roosevelt met with Abdul Aziz ibn Saud, King of Saudi Arabia. FDR was returning from the Yalta conference that divvied up Europe among the presumptive victors. One could say that the meetings between Roosevelt and Abdul Aziz on the USS *Quincy* in the Great Bitter Lake, part of the Suez Canal, did the same for the postwar Middle East. It was reportedly the first time that Adbul Aziz had ever left his country.

His family had consolidated power in the Arabian peninsula over a 200-year period, culminating in the seizure of the Islamic holy sites Mecca and Medina in 1924 and 1925, respectively. Around that same time, oil was discovered in the peninsula, and American oil conglomerate Saudi Aramco negotiated concessions with the House of Saud to explore and extract the precious resource.

The U.S. government grew more interested in securing access to this oil in the run-up to World War II and during the war. Great Britain had dominated much of the Persian Gulf region since the end of World War I, but Britain's long decline—in some respects sealed by World War II—opened the way for much closer ties between the United States and the Saudis.

It was an odd union, to the say the least. The U.S.–Saudi relationship always conflicted with Americans' stated commitment to democracy and human rights. Abdul Aziz and his successors were never elected as heads of state; the family forcibly seized power and has viciously repressed challenges to its rule ever since. The Saudis employ draconian punishments on criminals and miscreants, including public executions. They deny basic rights to women and persecute religious and ethnic minorities. In the 2017 Human Freedom Index, Saudi Arabia ranks a dismal 149th out of 159 countries scored, below Zimbabwe, Pakistan, and the Republic of Congo.[19] The Saudis also impose severe restrictions on the companies operating in their country, and they have even restricted U.S. government officials. Indeed, they have demanded that the United States alter *its* policies to conform with or accommodate the Kingdom's, though not often successfully.

The Saudis' behavior outside the Kingdom is equally problematic for the United States. On numerous occasions going back at least to the mid-1950s, the United States has become involved in a regional dispute to assuage Saudi fears, to tip the balance away from one of their rivals, and to generally affirm our commitment to their security. Many of these wars have ended badly or seem likely to do so (the war in Yemen is still ongoing).

Meanwhile, the Saudis' malign influence extends well outside of their immediate neighborhood. Early on during its rise to power, the House of Saud made common cause with the preachers of an austere strain of Islam known as Wahhabism, and the Saudis have helped promulgate Wahhabism globally ever since. Some of the preachers and adherents to Wahhabism ended up in Pakistan and Afghanistan as part of a global jihad to expel the Soviet infidels from Muslim lands. When they succeeded at that task (with considerable help from the United States), some of these jihadists turned their attention toward expelling other infidels from other Muslim lands. Many Americans are aware that 15 of the 19 September 11th hijackers were Saudis and that the operation was organized by the most notorious terrorist leader in recent history: Osama bin Laden, also a Saudi. Fewer are probably aware that bin Laden organized his transnational movement, al Qaeda ("the base"), chiefly to resist the presence of U.S. troops in the land of the two holy mosques (i.e., Saudi Arabia).[20]

In their essential book on the history of America's relations with numerous "perilous partners," Ted Galen Carpenter and Malou Innocent have this to say about the U.S.–Saudi alliance: it "played a major role in the region's radicalization and destabilizing disintegration" and "sacrificed America's commitment to liberalism for the sake of security and undermined both."[21]

But it wasn't the only alliance that did. For decades, the United States allied with a number of other brutal and autocratic regimes, and the results were often the same: undermining both U.S. security *and* U.S. values.

For example, the United States helped engineer a coup in 1953 that overthrew a democratically elected government in Iran and installed Mohammad Reza Pahlavi as shah—this time with unconstrained powers. The rationales for ousting Prime Minister Mohammed Mossadegh included the economic interests of Western oil companies who had seen their assets nationalized by Mossadegh's government. The Americans also feared that Mossadegh was growing too close to the Soviet Union.

There were some grounds for such suspicions, but the overthrow of a democratic leader left deep scars on the Iranian psyche and would ultimately come back to bite the United States. Although Pahlavi was one of the United States' most reliable allies in the 1950s, 60s, and 70s, he presided over a brutal and repressive government that routinely jailed, tortured, and executed political prisoners and dissidents. His secret police, SAVAK, was particularly notorious. Reputable groups such as Amnesty International reported such abuses, but U.S. officials largely ignored them. When the shah was deposed in a popular uprising in February 1979, many Iranians directed their anger at the United States.[22]

Nearly 40 years later, the religious zealots empowered by the anti-shah revolution continue to strangle human freedom in Iran. The country scored 154th out of 159 in the 2017 Human Freedom Index.[23]

Another example of a perilous partnership that has thwarted liberty is the U.S.–Egyptian alliance. When pro-democracy activists rose up in Egypt in 2011 to protest the decades-long rule of Hosni Mubarak and his cronies, many remembered the role that the United States had played in keeping Mubarak's regime in power. And for those who didn't, the "Made in USA" labels on the tear gas canisters launched at protesters in Cairo's Tahrir Square were timely reminders.

Mubarak, a former general in the Egyptian Air Force, had been vice president of Egypt at the time of Anwar Sadat's assassination in 1981. He assumed the presidency and held it for more than three decades. During his long reign, Egypt was the second-leading recipient of U.S. foreign assistance (after Israel). Billions of dollars flowed to the Egyptian military, which remained loyal to Mubarak until the bitter end. In the eyes of many Egyptians, the Obama administration's belated decision to cut Mubarak loose didn't absolve the United States of its sins of having supported him for decades.[24]

Sometimes it is truly necessary to ally with brutal dictators when the common enemies that we confront are even worse. That certainly explains the decision to side with Joseph Stalin against Adolf Hitler during World War II. Similarly, our Cold War–era alliances with autocratic regimes were justified, if not always justifiable, by the belief that Soviet tyranny was a threat to both global security and liberty.

But we should set a high bar. Carpenter and Innocent point to the need to maintain public support for U.S. foreign policy, calling on policymakers to honestly assess the issues at stake. They also call for candor about our partners.

Such candor has often been in short supply. As noted in the previous chapter, the United States has enormous latitude over when and whether to intervene abroad. But precisely because Americans are already so secure, mobilizing them to undertake foreign wars is difficult.

Difficult, but not impossible. Americans were willing to expend considerable effort to dislodge Nazi Germany and Imperial Japan in World War II. And most Americans were willing to tolerate alliances with brutal tyrants because the alternatives were far worse and because the security stakes—for the United States—were fairly obvious.

Most cases are not nearly as clear cut, however. If Americans believe that we are merely trading one petty despot for another, with only a marginal improvement for U.S. security or the cause of human rights, then they are ambivalent.

So U.S. leaders obfuscate. They shade the truth. They lie. They exaggerate the harm that might come if petty despot A stays in power. He's the next Hitler, they say. He's the next Mao. Therefore, we must help petty despot B.

And then they lie about the nature of petty despot B. He's not so bad. He's a democrat. He's our friend. He has the best interests of his people at heart. Sometimes, U.S. officials apparently believe their own lies.

Not every ally will be as odious as Stalin, but not every adversary will be as dangerous as Hitler. Further, when partnerships with authoritarian rulers or illiberal regimes are absolutely necessary, U.S. policymakers should limit cooperation to only the areas that are essential to achieving crucial goals.

The most important consideration, however, when it comes to alliances with shady associates is a careful assessment of the country's interests and geostrategic situation. We should be skeptical of the supposed need for entangling alliances in the first place, but especially skeptical when they lead us to sacrifice liberal values.

The United States should hold itself to the highest possible standards, in part because of our traditional role as the leading exemplar of liberal values globally, but also because our safety and security rarely hinges upon the support of allies. As Carpenter and Innocent observe in *Perilous Partners*, "With an enviable geographic position (weak and friendly neighbors to the north and south and vast oceans on both flanks), the largest economy in the world, a conventional military establishment far superior to any competitor, and a huge, sophisticated nuclear deterrent, the United States is probably the most secure great power in history."[25]

Generally speaking, we are safer than our leaders often lead us to believe, and our frequent interventions—often undertaken on behalf of our allies—are as likely to undermine U.S. security as to advance it. Our entanglements with authoritarian regimes often compound this problem, undermining both our security *and* our values.

Given that "U.S. leaders have extraordinary latitude to adopt policies that minimize America's involvement in quarrels in other parts of the world," they should be particularly wary of cozying up to unsavory regimes.[26] And they should consider all the possible costs, including the costs to our reputation, before they choose to ally with brutal, illiberal governments.

(11)

Forcing Freedom

In his July 4, 1821, address, John Quincy Adams warned that if the United States succumbed to the impulse to wage war against others who didn't adopt its views on human rights and effective governance, it would be no different from the empires of old. But he also believed that it could promote human freedom globally, by "the countenance of her voice, and the benignant sympathy of her example," without undermining freedom at home.[1]

Was Adams right? Could the United States advance the cause of liberty without resorting to force? Did it risk becoming an empire if it ignored his warnings and instead went "abroad in search of monsters to destroy"?

Many of Adams's contemporaries thought so. And several generations of American political leaders and statesmen invoked Adams's words as the ultimate guide for U.S. foreign policy.

But is it necessarily true today, nearly 200 years later? After all, the U.S. government has, on occasion, used force to spread liberty elsewhere without necessarily destroying it at home. For many Americans, Adams's words still ring true, but others doubt that they should apply today.

In those instances, when we consider whether and how to promote liberty abroad, we should turn instead to another famous figure from the 19th century: the great moral philosopher John Stuart Mill. A proud citizen of Great Britain at the height of its imperial glory, Mill didn't dwell on the possible harms that British imperialism might cause on British subjects at home. Instead, in his famous essay "A Few Words on Non-Intervention," published in 1859, Mill adopted a consequentialist approach. Presuming that classical liberals should wish to spread liberal ideas to the widest possible audience, was it wise to do so by force?

Generally speaking, Mill concluded, it was not.

Mill did not arrive at this conclusion on the basis of a narrow definition of national interest. Indeed, he seemed particularly disdainful of the impulse. In the essay, he takes aim at those who, when presented with an argument for foreign intervention, would invoke "this shabby refrain—'We do not interfere, because no English interest was involved'; 'We ought not interfere where no English interest is concerned.'" He further writes, "Of all attitudes which a nation can take up on the subject of intervention, the meanest and worst is to profess that it interferes only when it can serve its own objects by it."[2]

Of course, these same principles of noninterference do not apply when a nation's safety or vital interests are endangered. When an intervention is justified on grounds of self-defense, the intervening state should be granted wide latitude—so long as the evidence of grave danger or imminent attack is credible. No state in the 19th century would have been expected to suffer the first blow.

Nor would any state in this century, when the first blow in question might come via a thermonuclear weapon.

But Mill's Great Britain in the 19th century held itself to a higher standard with respect to interventions that were not strictly defensive in nature. Many Americans like to think that the United States continues this tradition. The American role in the world today as many U.S. officials have practiced it (or at least professed it) is to advance not merely the safety and security of all Americans but also the interests and well-being of mankind. The instinct is not entirely altruistic; many in the policymaking community believe that a more democratic, more rights-respecting, and more prosperous world will also be a more peaceful one. We produce safety for ourselves by producing it for others.

Of course, the United States does not always intervene on behalf of others. Nor did Great Britain always intervene in the 19th century. Mill explained that foreign intervention for the purpose of making people free should be limited to those who had taken up "arms for liberty" to throw off the yoke of foreign domination.

Mill therefore thought it unjust to support governments that were actively thwarting liberty. "A government which needs foreign support to enforce obedience of its own citizens," he wrote, "is one that ought not exist; and the assistance given to it by foreigners is hardly ever anything but the sympathy of one despotism over another." It seems obvious what Mill would think of U.S. support for numerous perilous partners over the years (see chapter 10).

Then there are the cases involving a group of people attempting to dislodge their indigenous government (in other words, not a foreign occupier). Iraqis struggling under the oppression of Saddam Hussein's tyranny in 2003 are a representative modern case.

Mill concluded that it was generally inappropriate to intervene in such instances. As he explained:

> If a people . . . does not value [liberty] sufficiently to fight for it, and maintain it against any force which can be mustered *within* the country . . . it is only a question in how few years or months that people will be enslaved. . . . Men become attached to that which they have long fought for and made sacrifices for . . . . And a contest in which many have been called on to devote themselves for their country, is a school in which they learn to value their country's interest above their own.[3]

Mill reiterated the exceptions to the norm of nonintervention: as always, cases of self-defense, and also intervention on behalf of foreign peoples held in subjugation by a third party. He explained that if liberating these people "struggling against a foreign yoke" would restore the balance for liberty and in favor of self-determination, another of his key principles, then foreign intervention might be warranted.[4]

Might be. But what might be justified according to moral principles might still be unwise. "Intervention to enforce non-intervention," Mill explained, "is always rightful, always moral, if not always prudent."[5] Mill's appreciation for unintended consequences, which predated Hayek by nearly a century (see chapter 8), undergirds his entire brief on behalf of nonintervention.

In his book *The Question of Intervention: John Stuart Mill and the Responsibility to Protect*, Michael Doyle reminds us of the "consequentialist character of the ethics of both nonintervention and intervention."[6] Echoing Mill, Doyle explains that "not every oppressive abuse that justifies a rebellion by locals justifies an intervention by foreigners. Humanitarian duties are contextual, and self-determination constrains humanitarian concerns."[7] Self-interest also comes into play. No one should expect the United States, or any other country, to gravely endanger its own security in the service of humanitarian principles.

When is it prudent, therefore, to avoid war for the cause of liberty, even when it might be justified to fight one? The question "Should we attempt to force freedom?" should be chiefly informed by another, simpler, question: "Can we?" Or still another: "Do we trust government leaders to have the pure intentions they claim in carrying out such avowedly moral crusades?" And also: "Do the limited and enumerated powers under the Constitution allow U.S. officials to wage such crusades on their own authority even if there are no concrete U.S. national security issues at stake?"

In the modern era, the legitimate rationales for the use of force include a view of universal human rights that goes well beyond Mill's 19th-century conception. Much of Mill's thinking ought to remain in the past. He justified continued rule by foreign colonial masters over "uncivilized" peoples or "barbarous" governments, a blunt reminder of the pervasive racism that undergirds imperialism. But contemporary conceptions of when humanitarian intervention is justified are flawed in ways that Mill would appreciate.

As Mill taught, we should not confine ourselves merely to considerations of what interventions are *permissible* on normative grounds, presuming flawless execution. We should also keep in mind whether such interventions are likely to be *effective*. Will an intervention explicitly undertaken to deliver liberty to an oppressed people or advance the cause of human rights actually produce that result? Will it grant some number of people the ability to govern themselves? And if it affords them that opportunity but they ultimately fail to realize it, is that their fault or the fault of the intervener?

Mill expected that most such interventions, even if they were morally permissible, would fail. He anticipated that one of three scenarios was likely to transpire, and the end result of all three was not freedom. In the first instance, the fragile political order fails to adapt to the change in regime, and civil war ensues. In the second instance, the intervening party determines that the newly liberated people are not ready to govern themselves and installs an indigenous strongman. This hasn't created liberty; it has merely replaced one ruler with another in the same illiberal system. In the third and final scenario, the foreign intervener, reluctant to install a local strongman but chastened by the likelihood that violence will erupt without one, decides to stay. But this hasn't created liberty, either. It has merely supplanted an indigenous illiberal government with a foreign one. The imperial overlord, whether he's called a viceroy or an administrator of the occupational authority, might believe in liberal values. He might enact laws and regulations respecting universal human rights, including gender equality and equal protections for religious and ethnic minorities. But even a liberal imperial administrator defies another key liberal principle: self-determination.

Recall the scene from the Academy Award–winning film *Gandhi*, in which the leader for Indian independence implores the British colonial administrators to leave the subcontinent.

Kinnoch: With respect, Mr. Gandhi, without British administration, this country would be reduced to chaos.

Gandhi: Mr. Kinnoch, I beg you to accept that there is no people on earth who would not prefer their own bad government to the good government of an alien power.

British Officer #1: Oh, my dear sir, India is British. We're hardly an alien power.

Lord Chelmsford: Mr. Gandhi, even if His Majesty could wave all other considerations, he has a duty to the millions of his Muslim subjects who are a minority in this realm. And experience suggests that his troops and his administration are essential in order to secure the peace.

Gandhi: All nations contain religious minorities. Like other countries, ours will have its problems. But they will be ours—not yours.[8]

The actual history of postcolonial India confirmed many of the former British masters' fears, including horrific violence between minority Muslims and majority Hindus, but the British were not in a particularly strong position to protest. After all, the British raj had perpetrated atrocities, too. In the end, many Muslims opted for partition over unity, creating the states of Pakistan and East Pakistan (later Bangladesh). It was, as the British predicted, chaos. But it was, as Gandhi replied, their own chaos.

Confirming Mill's suspicions is Doyle's research into the question of whether liberal-led foreign interventions between 1815 and 2003 produced lasting liberty. Less than one in five delivered the benefits intended. The remaining cases lapsed back into "civil war, a deepened autocracy, or imperial rule."[9]

Political scientists Alexander Downes and Jonathan Monten reached similar conclusions. Their study of foreign-imposed regime changes (FIRCs) in the 20th century found that very few such interventions resulted in stable democracies; critical preconditions must already exist in the target country and the intervener must take concrete steps to implement democratic reforms. In countries with heterogeneous populations, poor economic conditions, and weak or nonexistent democratic institutions or traditions, a FIRC is likely to result in civil war. The few FIRCs that succeeded involved getting states that had previously democratized on their own back on track. The successful cases also tended to be wealthier countries with more homogenous populations.

Downes and Monten issued a warning to policymakers tempted by the allure of "precision airpower and remotely piloted drone aircraft":

> Regime change may appear to be a low-cost option for powerful democracies such as the United States in the twenty-first century because potential targets are weak

states, but looks can be deceiving. Democracy is unlikely to take root in these places, and the United States might find itself drawn into protracted quagmires such as Afghanistan and Iraq.[10]

Even a textbook postconflict occupation, one in which the occupying army commits no egregious errors and goes out of its way to protect civilians, risks engendering hostility and dependency. When Georgetown University professor David Edelstein surveyed the historical record of postwar occupations from the time of Napoleon to the present day, he found that most such occupations have failed. In those that succeeded, Edelstein identified three common factors. One, the occupied population must recognize the need for an occupation in terms of providing for internal security. Two, both the occupying power and the occupied population must perceive a common external threat to the occupied territory. And three, an occupation is likely to generate less opposition when the occupying power makes a credible guarantee that it will withdraw and return control to an indigenous government in a timely manner. Absent these three conditions, Edelstein explains, occupying powers will face the dilemma of either evacuating prematurely and increasing the probability that later reintervention will be necessary, or sustaining the occupation at an unacceptable cost.[11]

Despite this research and the United States' unhappy experience in Iraq and Afghanistan, few among the foreign policy elite have been dissuaded from urging regime change. In 2011, the Obama administration secured a UN Security Council resolution authorizing air strikes to protect Libyan civilians threatened by Muammar Qaddafi. The mission quickly evolved into regime change with the United States, NATO, and a handful of Arab states carrying out a concerted air campaign focused on Qaddafi's forces. The longtime ruler met his end in September of that year. Secretary of State Hillary Clinton, channeling her inner Julius Caesar, quipped, "We came, we saw, he died."[12]

But it wasn't that simple. Within a few years, Libya was a basket case. Alan Kuperman, in a policy brief for Harvard's prestigious Belfer Center, concluded that "NATO's action magnified the conflict's duration about sixfold and its death toll at least seven-fold . . . while also exacerbating human rights abuses, humanitarian suffering, Islamic radicalism, and weapons proliferation in Libya and its neighbors."[13]

The Libyan episode and its aftermath speaks to the third leading reason why it is unwise to adopt a foreign policy based on forcing freedom: even well-intended interventions can fail, and even well-executed ones can harm the intervening state's security.

The fact that Libya is an utter disaster doesn't necessarily mean that the intervention was neither permissible nor just. In many respects, it was more legal under international law than most other recent interventions because it had UN Security Council authorization. Its legality under U.S. law, on the other hand, was questionable at best. The operation exceeded the time limits set forth in the War Powers Resolution, and the Obama administration never sought—and Congress never granted—the authority to use force. Meanwhile, the president never claimed that the intervention was advancing a vital national security interest.

Legality aside, however, what happened in Libya does validate the concerns that Vice President Joe Biden, Secretary of Defense Robert Gates, and nearly all senior military officers had that the intervention was unwise. It was unlikely to achieve its stated goals, including protecting innocent human lives, at reasonable cost, and it was inconsistent with U.S. national security interests. A few even warned—presciently, though tragically—that the chaos likely to ensue after Qaddafi's ouster would harm U.S. interests and even threaten U.S. security.[14]

And so it did. The collapse of order in Libya since 2011 created a void that terrorist organizations were happy to fill. In early 2016, as the Islamic State captured territory there, U.S. and European officials grew so worried that the militants might have yet another stronghold where they could plot attacks against Western interests that there were urgent calls for new air strikes. Some politicians even considered the possibility of sending U.S. ground troops.

The unhappy experience in Libya in 2011 appears to have informed the Obama administration's refusal to intervene decisively in Syria in 2012. And when it seemed poised to do so in the late summer of 2013, the American people rose up in opposition, inundating Washington with phone calls and emails telling their representatives to stay out of yet another Middle Eastern civil war.

That is as it should be. The burden of proof should always be on those making the case for intervention. The default position is, and should be, nonintervention. Mill's wise counsel still holds.

12

The Global Economy

A nation's vital interests include more than its physical security. Citizens do not merely want to feel safe from danger; they also want to live fulfilling lives. Thus, prosperity is also a core national interest. Producers want access to foreign markets, and consumers also benefit from substantial foreign trade. Modern economies can't thrive if the global economy is frail or faltering.

As noted in chapter 5, philosophers and statesmen have long believed that trade and economic interdependence are crucial drivers of peace. And yet despite close economic ties, the countries of Europe waged war with one another not long after Norman Angell predicted that it would be foolish to do so. Ever since, skeptics of the capitalist peace have pointed to World War I, and later World War II, as definitive proof that Angell was badly mistaken.

Nothing could be further from the truth. Angell did not declare that war was obsolete, but rather that it should be. Although most European countries descended into a maelstrom of violence in August 1914 and were joined by others later, that does not negate the validity of Angell's thesis. On the contrary, his claim that war was unlikely to achieve favorable results at reasonable cost was almost certainly proved by the chaos that ensued: the war lasted far longer than any of the combatants expected, and it was the most ruinous in all of human history. Until the next world war, that is.

Since the second world war, the United States has had a major hand in setting the rules of the game, and the U.S. government—and the U.S. military—often takes a leading role in punishing those who disobey.

Primacists assert that U.S. military dominance protects the global economy by reducing the risk of war or tamping down wars that it fails to stop. They claim that a global military posture, and especially security commitments to wealthy allies, reduces the likelihood of conflict. Wars—or the mere fear of them—would roil skittish markets; by stopping wars, the hegemon allows markets to flourish and grow.

It is true that U.S. military primacy has coincided with a decline in interstate conflict, but it is hardly the only factor behind the drop in violence. Meanwhile, the global economy *has* reaped a healthy peace dividend. Total military spending as a share of global GDP has fallen from an average of 5.1 percent between 1972 and 1990 to 2.5 percent in the decade after 9/11.[1] The vast majority of countries are spending less on their militaries, which leaves them with more money to spend on other more productive investments.

This is likely to have long-term negative repercussions, however, especially for the United States. "The cost of maintaining global public goods catches up to the sole superpower," notes political scientist Daniel Drezner. "Other countries free-ride off the hege-mon, allowing them to grow faster. Technologies diffuse from the hegemonic power to the rest of the world, facilitating catch-up."[2]

The costs aren't merely measured in treasure. They're also mea-sured in blood. The U.S. military has been engaged in a cycle of persistent conflict for nearly a generation.

It is questionable whether the United States' willingness to wage war in the past quarter century has generated economic benefits, for the world or for Americans. Indeed, a number of recent U.S. military interventions have done more harm than good, upsetting established political systems, threatening regional markets, and sowing doubts about the future that discourage investment and entrepreneurial risk-taking.

This is particularly unfortunate because the world economy doesn't need much policing. Maintaining U.S. access to global markets isn't hard, either, considering the sheer size and power of the U.S. economy. Sellers want access to buyers. New businesses around the world are hungry for capital. The United States has a lot of both.

In another respect, Americans aren't particularly unique. Most countries benefit from access to global markets and thus have no desire to disrupt the free flow of goods and services. On the con-trary, they have a powerful interest to defend it. The few actors who might wish to upend the global economy lack the power to do so. They can cause temporary disruptions, but the market adapts.

In a dynamic economy, producers seek new ways to profit. Sup-ply chains are durable and resilient. In extreme cases, for example, when pirates are preying on ships in the open sea or when conflict threatens to close narrow straits or waterways, ships may alter course to circumvent these dangerous areas. Suppliers' costs may rise, but consumers may be willing to pay more and will substitute other products if they are not.[3]

The Capitalist Peace

There are other reasons to question whether the United States must maintain peace in order to facilitate commerce. It is possible that the causal arrows flow in the other direction.

Many 19th-century liberals believed that trade was conducive to peace. The world wars damaged this notion, since the belligerents had enjoyed extensive commercial relations in the antebellum periods, but recent research has affirmed classical liberalism's basic insights. The political scientist Erik Gartzke places particular importance on human freedom as a cause for peace—more important than trade, per se, and far more significant than Kantian democracy. "Economic freedom," Gartzke writes, "is one of the rare factors that generally discourages conflict among nations."

"Democracy is desirable for many reasons," Gartzke continues, "but policies that encourage, or even seek to impose, representative government are unlikely to contribute directly to international peace." Prosperity is the necessary precondition to achieve stable and secure democracies, and it is "sufficient to produce peace." Accordingly, "the best foreign policy," Gartzke explains, "is one that enhances and extends capitalism."[4]

Gartzke affirms the two pillars of Angell's argument. First, he agrees that economic development makes wars of conquest unprofitable. And second, he concurs with Angell's assessment that greater economic integration among and between states "makes it easier to acquire goods and services through trade and harder to avoid unsettling investors through warfare." But Angell focused too narrowly on economic gain as the primary or even sole motive for conflict. Greed was only one of Hobbes's three causes for war; equally important were fear and honor. Thus, Gartzke concludes, "the capitalist peace offered by Angell and other classical liberals is not wrong but incomplete."[5]

Mutually desired things, from coveted land to scarce resources, may be profitably traded or bought and sold, but they might also provide occasion for wars to be fought. Uncertainty is critical. The contestants may misconstrue or misunderstand what the other party is willing to accept in a negotiated settlement or what they will do to secure similar ends if they perceive themselves to be at a disadvantage.

Economic freedom can be conducive to peace for at least two reasons. First, when people are free to move themselves or their money, governments are incentivized to create the conditions that make people want to stay put. In that context, wars, which are generally bad for business, are especially harmful when people and capital are mobile. Unsurprisingly, notes Gartzke, citing work by the Hoover Institution's Bruce Bueno de Mesquita, "the use of force abroad is often associated with a decline in domestic investment and with outflows of capital."[6] Second, modern economies that rely on intellectual and financial capital see little value in wars of foreign occupation. The impulse, therefore, is to avoid wars that might require such missions—and many wars do. Having invested blood and treasure to topple a foreign government or punish a regime for its misbehavior, interveners are reluctant to risk seeing it lapse back into its bad old ways; the temptation is to never leave.

The Continued Benefits of Trade

We should challenge the view that the United States must police the globe in order to ensure that the international economy functions efficiently. Businesses and consumers do not require the U.S. military to provide access to foreign markets. But we should also affirm the value of trade in and of itself. Many people around the world today need convincing.

Some Americans, for example, doubt that foreign trade is all that important. The U.S. consumer market is large enough to sustain demand for U.S. products, and the country is blessed with ample natural resources. Still others see trade as a zero-sum game. As they see it, explains Cato's Dan Ikenson, "exports are Team America's points; imports are the foreign team's points; the trade account is the scoreboard and a bilateral deficit means the U.S. team is losing . . . and it's losing because the foreign team cheats." Almost every aspect of this view is incorrect. We need a better case for free trade.[7]

Zero-sum thinking flies in the face of a mountain of empirical evidence proving the benefits of specialization and comparative advantage. It is, in short, economically illiterate.

It's also dangerous.

To return to the mercantilism of the 18th and 19th century would consign us all to slow or even negative growth, and increase the likelihood of conflict. Global engagement through trade enhances our prosperity *and* our safety.

The philosophers and intellectuals of the 19th and early 20th century imagined that trade was conducive to peace. Modern scholars have expanded and elaborated on these arguments, armed with empirical evidence.

Freedom is the key to the capitalist peace. Wars are less likely to occur in places where individuals and businesses can easily move their money or even themselves. If war does break out, the mobility of labor and capital leaves the warring parties with less than they started—often much less. This should, and does, serve as a powerful deterrent to those tempted to initiate violence.

The world has witnessed a vast expansion of its productive capacity since the end of the second world war. We take our modern conveniences for granted, and we are generally unaware of how much better our situation is over that of the generations that came before us or even of ourselves when we were younger. The changes have been so gradual as to be imperceptible.[8]

The functioning of the global economy has also improved. This system, sustained by human action but not by human design, is more resilient and dynamic than ever. But it is also more vital than ever. No country can truly thrive as an island, disconnected from trade with the rest of the world.

Still, the advocates for peaceful global engagement through trade and mutually beneficial exchange have a hard task before them. They straddle the fence between two warring camps. One side argues that global peace and prosperity require the United States to maintain a costly global military presence, to pledge to defend other countries from dangers, and to maintain access to global markets against all threats. The other side rejects the global public goods argument in its entirety. Surveying the high costs and dubious benefits of America's many wars, they call for an unabashed nationalism that puts America first. And, anxious about the ability of U.S. firms to compete in a global marketplace, they would throw up a metaphorical wall to keep out foreign goods and an actual wall to keep out foreign labor.

But although Donald Trump tapped into this isolationist sentiment and shocked the world, it isn't certain that his foreign policy vision will survive even his own presidency. A majority of Americans are supportive of global engagement, and young people are even more internationalist than their parents and grandparents. They value the cultural exchange that comes from frequent interactions with people from diverse backgrounds.[9]

On the other hand, if global engagement is seen as synonymous with inconclusive military entanglements abroad and fiscal ruin at home, then we can expect that more Americans will demand a sharp turn inward. If U.S. foreign policy elites refuse to change course, tinkering around the margins but still sending U.S. troops to fight costly wars of choice while sticking U.S. taxpayers with the bill, then we might see even stronger isolationist sentiments, tinged with nativism and xenophobia.

Peaceful, voluntary interaction through trade has been the touchstone of American foreign policy since the nation's founding, and it is a pattern that many other countries have since emulated. It would be particularly tragic if America turned its back on the global economy just as the rest of the world was opening up to it.

(13)

New Rules

Any nation with vast power will be tempted to use it, and the United States is exceptional in that regard only to the extent that its power appears, on the surface at least, to be nearly unlimited.[1] The United States is capable of intervening militarily anywhere on the planet, with only a moment's notice. The U.S. Navy maintains a regular forward presence in the Pacific and Atlantic Oceans and in nearly every major body of water accessible from the major oceans, including the Persian Gulf and the South and East China Seas. Small, weak countries dare not contemplate intervening in distant disputes that have little direct impact on their security. The risk that assets directed elsewhere might be lost or otherwise unavailable for defense generally keeps those assets nearby.

Relieved of such concerns, the United States has long entertained requests for assistance and doesn't much worry that a naval squadron sent to help typhoon victims in the Indian Ocean or earthquake survivors in Pakistan will be needed closer to home. Other peoples in need or nations who feel threatened by their neighbors regularly appeal for help. And Uncle Sam has often responded.

Be that as it may, this book has documented the many reasons why Americans should restrict their government's impulse to intervene militarily abroad. And if the United States exercises greater restraint, the world should move to a posture of resilience and self-reliance, becoming progressively less dependent on an Uncle Sam that is considerably more reticent to use force.

But constraining America's interventionist impulses will be difficult. With great power, as the Spider-Man comic books and films remind us, comes great responsibility. The impulse to use this power seems almost overwhelming.

It won't be easy to transition from the unipolar order to a more resilient, multilateral one for other reasons. Other countries will be expected to bear additional costs to defend themselves and their interests, and they would prefer to spend those moneys on other things. They will continue, therefore, to call for U.S. assistance and to claim that they are incapable of doing more. Every time Washington responds favorably to such calls, the impetus for action on the part of other countries abates.

Resistance will also come from some quarters within the United States. Whereas most Americans believe that the U.S. military should be focused chiefly on defending the United States, and they routinely tell pollsters that they want the U.S. government to focus more attention to problems at home, the foreign policy elite remains fully invested in the current hegemonic grand strategy. So long as the United States possesses the military to defend others as well as itself, they will push for military intervention wherever they deem it necessary. Better that the United States intervene, they will say, than for others to do so.

There is also the matter of that transitionary period—that indeterminate period of time, be it a few years or a few decades—when U.S. power remains dominant, and other countries will not yet have the capabilities to fill the void. During that period in particular, the United States must establish clear and stringent standards concerning when and whether it will deploy U.S. troops into harm's way. These rules will signal to both the American people and, just as important, American allies what is expected of them.

Consider the U.S. National Security Interests at Stake

The first and most important message to be communicated to the American people, and the people of the world, is that the U.S. military exists to defend U.S. core national security interests. It should not be in the business of defending other countries that can and should defend themselves. Therefore, the United States must not risk the lives of U.S. service members unless *there is a vital U.S. national security interest at stake.*

This would seem to be both rather obvious and rather broad given that U.S. national security interests can be—and have been—defined quite expansively. But we should not confuse vital national security interests with important but nonvital interests or peripheral ones. Protecting the physical security of the territory of the United States and the safety of its people are vital national security interests. Many of the tasks that U.S. policymakers assign to our military are only tangentially, if at all, directed to those ends. Some are important but can be advanced by peaceful means. Still others can safely be abandoned.

Consider that U.S. national security as defined above has very rarely been threatened in the last few decades. A few al Qaeda terrorists wreaked havoc on September 11, 2001, but al Qaeda on its best day never approached the scale of death and destruction that a nuclear-armed Soviet Union was capable of unleashing on its worst. Terrorists and mass murderers can unleash mayhem in a given place, or a few places. They can cause harm. But they cannot destroy the country. They cannot invade and occupy it. They cannot extinguish millions of lives in an instant. They cannot take away our liberty, alter our system of government, or destroy all of our property.

Having clarified what is meant by vital national security interest, we can see that these criteria are quite limiting—more stringent, for example, than the Reagan-era Weinberger-Powell Doctrine.[2] The guidelines, first spelled out in 1984, held that U.S. troops should not be sent overseas "unless the particular engagement or occasion is deemed vital to our national interest *or that of our allies.*"[3] By effectively equating U.S. national interests with those of allies, the Weinberger-Powell Doctrine allowed for a range of interventions that would not be considered valid under the criteria spelled out here. Rather than assume that U.S. interests are synonymous with those of our allies and that U.S. troops should risk their lives to protect them as though they were protecting U.S. interests here at home, we should closely scrutinize all of our obligations to our allies, formal or otherwise. Americans should consider whether these interests are, in fact, on par with vital U.S. security interests, and consider under what circumstances—and, crucially, on whose authority—these obligations might translate into a formal commitment of U.S. military personnel into combat.

Clear National Consensus

Libertarians, jealous as we are about constraining the power of the state, should be particularly wary of circumstances that circumvent public debate over policy matters of great significance. In the case of military intervention abroad, the American people must understand why they are being asked to send their sons and daughters, brothers and sisters, husbands and wives, to risk their lives abroad. And, crucially, they must have a say in when and whether to do so. In short, the U.S. military should not be engaged in combat operations overseas unless there is *a clear national consensus* behind the mission.

Although modern technology allows the public to weigh in on matters great and small, and in near real-time (think *American Idol* or *Dancing with the Stars*), we need not rely on Twitter polls to ascertain whether the American people support the use of force. We need only use the tool written into the Constitution: the stipulation that Congress alone, not the president, possesses the power to take the country to war. James Madison once called this provision the most important of the entire document. Strictly adhering to this rule when considering the use of force abroad would help restore the balance between the executive and legislative branches. The separation of powers with ambition counteracting ambition, as Madison explained in *Federalist* 51, has largely served to preserve individual liberty here at home.

The Founders established a republic, not a direct democracy. They did not anticipate or desire that important decisions would be settled by plebiscite. They did, however, intend that citizens would convey their wishes to their elected representatives. The

Founders further believed that it would be difficult to build consensus around any particular policy, especially decisions as momentous as war and peace.

But Congress has regularly evaded its constitutional obligations, especially since the early Cold War. Harry Truman referred to U.S. intervention in Korea as a police action. Congress never declared war on Vietnam; Lyndon Johnson used the Tonkin Gulf Resolution as a license for a massive expansion of the U.S. role in Southeast Asia. George H. W. Bush secured a congressional Authorization for Use of Military Force against Iraq in 1991, and his son George W. Bush followed a similar path in 2002.

In other words, although the U.S. military has been in an almost continuous state of war for decades, few in Congress have ever weighed in publicly on the wisdom or folly of any particular foreign conflict. It isn't clear that they even know that they're going on. Most representatives and senators are content to criticize the president when foreign wars go badly and take credit when they go well—and without ever having to cast a vote. Some now interpret UN Security Council resolutions or Article 5 of the NATO Treaty as obligating the United States to wage war without explicit authorization from Congress or any meaningful public debate.[4] This is unacceptable. The authority to deploy U.S. forces abroad should never be predelegated to circumvent the Congress—and by extension, the people—of the United States.

Understand the Costs—and How to Pay Them

Restoring the Congress's proper role in determining when and whether to go to war will not be enough. We must also *understand the costs of war and know how we will pay them* before we choose violence.

We cannot accurately gauge popular support for a given military intervention overseas if the case for war is based on unrealistic expectations of the likely costs. These costs must be based on reasonable estimates by military experts, not on the best-case scenarios that are promulgated by advocates for war. We need no more talk of "cakewalks," and we should never again pretend that oil revenues will cover the costs of war and thus that American taxpayers won't have to pay anything at all.[5] There is no such thing as a free lunch, and there is certainly no such thing as a free war.

Understanding these costs up front is essential to ensuring that popular support for the wars can survive temporary setbacks. This is difficult enough for wars that do not advance a clear national security interest. The American people were ambivalent about the humanitarian mission in Somalia initiated by George H. W. Bush and then expanded under Bill Clinton in 1992 and 1993, respectively. What little support this well-intentioned but poorly thought-out operation had evaporated when Americans saw the true costs play out in the streets of Mogadishu. One *Black Hawk Down* incident was one too many for a mission that was not essential to preserving U.S. national security.

But we can't ignore the costs of wars sold to the American people on the grounds of national security. For one thing, the national security rationales can be deliberately misconstrued. Sometimes, intelligence purporting to find an imminent threat is simply wrong. The costs of taking action, therefore, must be weighed against the benefits. And if the costs are too high or the benefits are dubious, other approaches short of war may be preferable.

That is certainly what most Americans now think of the Iraq war. The Bush administration marketed the war as a noble mission to depose a brutal dictator with a functioning nuclear program and ties to al Qaeda. It capitalized on the public's fears after 9/11 and tapped into the understandable thirst for revenge. But the public's support for the Iraq venture collapsed when they learned the truth about Saddam's meager capabilities, and sunk even further when they appreciated just how costly the war had become. When al Qaeda affiliates emerged in the chaos that ensued after Saddam's overthrow, the true costs of that war became clear for all but the most closed-minded to see.

James Madison was sensitive to the possibility that even popular wars might prove more costly than wise. Whereby some speak blithely of democratic peace, Madison was not so naive. He was aware that man's passions, once aroused, might be more amplified than tempered by the agitations of his neighbors. He worried that wars precipitated by the public's desire for honor or revenge were every bit as dangerous to liberty as wars started by princes or kings. And he never forgot that war, with all of its horrible side effects for life and liberty, was never to be preferred for its own sake over peace. He sought, therefore, other ways to restrain the public's occasional enthusiasm for violence.

The best mechanism, he surmised, would be to subject "the will of the society to the reasons of the society."[6] People must be made aware that their actions have consequences; they must be cognizant of not only what they might gain, but also what they might be expected to give up.

Deficit spending allows the federal government to avoid consideration of such tradeoffs. Politicians are able to make promises in the here and now, the bills coming due long after they've left office or left this life. Though such expenditures might be justifiable in periods of genuine emergency, Washington has become adept at stretching the original meaning of that word past the breaking point. We need a reset. The word "emergency" can no longer be used as a cover for the government to spend whatever it wants, whenever it wants.

Madison's preferred solution was that "each generation should be made to bear the burden of its own wars, instead of carrying them on at the expense of other generations." In other words, no wars on credit. The best approach was pay as you go. If the advocates for war are forced to frame their solution to a given foreign challenge in terms of costs, they should also be forced to spell out what other expenditures should be cut or taxes raised to pay for their war. Some lament that hawks always seem to win, and there is evidence to suggest that they often do. But when their priorities are seen to conflict with the priorities of others, we can be confident that they will prevail less often.[7]

Clear and Obtainable Military Objectives

The next criterion is closely tied to the previous one. We cannot establish the likely costs of war and certainly cannot assess those costs in comparison with other solutions to a given problem if we can't clearly articulate ahead of time what, exactly, we are asking our troops to do. We should not send troops into harm's way without a set of *clear and obtainable military objectives.* What is the military's mission? Is that mission reasonably attainable? And lastly, how will we know when that mission is complete and, therefore, when the troops can come home? Every plan for getting into a war must have an equally detailed plan for getting out.

Such questions, as well as the earlier criteria with respect to costs, don't apply when a country's survival is at stake. The Soviets didn't ask for an exit strategy when the Nazis were plunging into the heart of the Motherland. They just fought. They suffered horrific losses, and they likely never stopped to consider how they would repay those costs after the war was over. They just hoped that the war didn't end with their total annihilation.

But the rules discussed here pertain to wars of choice, the types of wars that the United States has been fighting for the past half century. Once the advocates for war have demonstrated that a war is necessary to secure vital U.S. interests, and once they have secured public support for the mission, including an agreement to pay its costs, they must then spell out the military's mission.

In the modern era, it is usually insufficient to offer a strategy to achieve military victory over an offending regime or faction without also considering what comes after. In order for the war to be considered a net positive for U.S. vital national security interests, we must have high confidence that the regime or group that replaces the defeated forces represents a marked improvement over that which came before. Ensuring that such a transition occurs, that the right people fill the vacuum left behind and that they can hold onto power, can take a considerable amount of time.

This is what then–Secretary of State Colin Powell was talking about when he made reference to what has since been known as the Pottery Barn principle: "You break it, you buy it." Pottery Barn doesn't actually have such a policy, nor did Powell reference the store in his remarks. But what Powell actually said to President Bush in August 2002, recounted in Bob Woodward's book *Plan of Attack*, is important nonetheless. If Bush moved forward with this war, Powell explained, he would "be the proud owner of twenty-five million people." He went on, "You will own all their hopes, aspirations, problems. . . . It's going to suck the oxygen out of everything." He and other military leaders understand that wars don't stop when the shooting does, or when the president declares "Mission accomplished."

Powell understood, perhaps in ways that civilians who have never served in the military can't, that it is rather easy for politicians to start wars, but the troops are on the hook to end them—provided that the orders they are given can actually be carried out. Policymakers must explicitly account for the tendency of war to drag on for years or more and must plan for an acceptable exit. It's critical to know how our troops will get out, before we decide to send them in.

Use of Force as a Last Resort

The four criteria above are not enough to establish war's legitimacy or the wisdom of waging it. The American people will support the use of force when national security interests are at stake, but that doesn't mean that the use of force is necessary or acceptable. After all, many modern nation-states, and especially the United States, have the ability to wreak unimaginable horror on a massive scale. That obviously doesn't imply that they have a right to do so. Thus, the fifth and final rule concerning war and lesser forms of military intervention: force should be *used only as a last resort* and only after we have exhausted the other means for resolving a particular national security threat.

The point is, one hopes, rather banal—informed by centuries-old concepts of justice. Civilized societies abhor war, even wars that are waged for the right reasons and that adhere to standards set forth by just war theory. War is, and all wars are, a failure—a failure to resolve disputes by peaceful means. And the uncertainty of war demands that it should never be entered into lightly, or for trivial reasons.

Because of U.S. policymakers' enormous—practically limitless—capacity for waging war, they have a particularly unique obligation to remember that war is a last resort.

Not all U.S. officials have felt that way. The Bush administration lawyer John Yoo, who authored memos which purported to give legal cover to the plainly illegal torture of terrorism suspects, once said that in light of the supposedly uniquely dangerous threats confronting us today, "we should not . . . adopt a warmaking process that contains a built-in presumption against the use of force abroad."[8]

Actually, we should. The supposed dangers are precisely that: we do not live in a uniquely dangerous world. Americans today enjoy a measure of safety that our ancestors would envy and that our contemporaries do. Given this state of affairs, we should be extremely reluctant to intervene abroad when our vital interests are not directly threatened, when the public isn't on board, when the costs are unclear or exorbitant, when the military mission is murky or unobtainable, or when we have not yet exhausted other means for dealing with a difficult problem.

The purpose of these criteria—or *any* criteria, for that matter—should be to put the burden of proof back on the advocates for war. "Because we can" is not an adequate answer to the question "Why should we wage war in this country at this time?"

We always can. That is the nature of the U.S. military. Any military large enough to defend the vital national security interests of the vast United States of America will also be capable of intervening militarily abroad.

But that doesn't mean that we should.

(14)

Promised Land

When Chinese protesters took to the streets of Beijing in April 1989, some of the mostly young men and women took their inspiration from a distant country that many of them had never visited. In Tiananmen Square, in the shadow of the Great Hall of the People, the protesters assembled a makeshift statue in the shape of a woman, holding aloft a torch. Assembled from Styrofoam and papier-mâché, and constructed around a wire and metal frame, it seemed to bear a resemblance to a famous statue in New York Harbor.

Nearly 14 years later, another group of people were tearing down a statue, this one constructed of sturdier material. In Baghdad's Firdos Square, Iraqis swung sledgehammers at the concrete base of a 39-foot-tall Saddam Hussein. Eventually the massive bronze statue came down, in full view of international journalists lodged at the nearby Palestine Hotel. Broadcast worldwide, the images fed hopes that the Iraqi people, freed from Hussein's brutal rule, would quickly turn their focus away from destroying the symbols of the past and instead begin building a modern, liberal democracy for the future.

After watching the statue fall on television, Secretary of Defense Donald Rumsfeld talked to reporters. "The scenes of free Iraqis celebrating in the streets, riding American tanks . . . are breathtaking," he said. "One cannot help but think of the fall of the Berlin Wall and the collapse of the Iron Curtain."[1]

Not every regime change operation involves the use of force. Some governments step aside willingly, anxious to avoid bloodshed. On other occasions, peaceful protests turn violent. In late 2013, for example, Ukrainians assembled in Kiev's *Maidan Nezalezhnosti* (Independence Square) to protest President Viktor Yanukovych's decision to withdraw from an Association Agreement with the European Union that would have drawn Ukraine closer to Europe and away from Russia. Many saw Russian president Vladimir Putin's hand behind the Ukrainian leader's change of heart. Suspicions only deepened when Yanukovych eventually fled Ukraine for Russia.

But when Russian intelligence leaked an intercepted phone conversation between U.S. officials appearing to call for Yanukovych's overthrow, musing about which successors should lead the government that came after, some alleged that the entire Maidan uprising was an American-run operation.[2]

Such allegations are not as absurd as they might seem. After all, the U.S. government has engaged in a number of such operations since the start of the Cold War. Dov Levin, a researcher at Carnegie Mellon University, cataloged 81 cases between 1946 and 2000 in which the United States attempted to influence a foreign election. That's on top of the times the United States has played a more active role in overthrowing existing governments.

In Iran in 1953, Guatemala in 1954, and Chile in 1973, for example, seemingly spontaneous popular uprisings were—the world later learned—supported by the CIA or other entities backed by the U.S. government. These actions didn't so much reflect the will of the people as the subversion of it.[3]

One of the many tragic side effects of these past actions is that they now cast doubt on the enduring popularity of liberalism. Invariably, critics and scolds allege that an American hand is lurking behind every faint flowering of democracy or human rights, as if people around the world can't actually want more freedom unless Uncle Sam tells them to want it.

But there was no CIA operating in 1789 when Parisians stormed the Bastille. There were no American agents in Saint-Domingue (modern-day Haiti) when Toussaint Louverture led a slave insurrection that eventually secured independence from France. In the 1790s, the United States was in no position to intervene in a country several hundred miles from its shores. It remained unable or unwilling to assist those wishing to overthrow autocratic, tyrannical, or merely despotic governments for much of its history.

So how is it that liberal ideas have spread around the world? What role has the United States played? And what role should it play in the future? This final chapter explores these questions.

* * *

Historian Walter McDougall casts the history of U.S. foreign policy since its founding as a contrast between the Old and New Testaments of the Bible. In the Old Testament, Jerusalem stood out as an example for others to follow. Israel was the Promised Land, populated by a chosen people. So too would America, the New Israel, be a promised land of liberty. America's Founders and early statesmen—George Washington, James Madison, Thomas Jefferson, and John Quincy Adams—defined American exceptionalism by what the new nation was at home rather than by what it did abroad. They expected the United States to avoid entangling alliances, remain neutral in Europe's wars, and maintain contact with the rest of the world through commerce and cultural exchange.[4]

Starting in the late 19th century, the nation's leaders took their foreign policy cues from the crusading spirit of the New Testament. The early Christians saw it as their religious duty to proselytize the faith and rescue sinners and nonbelievers from eternal damnation. In this spirit, the United States became a crusader state, committed to uplifting the uncivilized few who lacked the knowledge and wisdom to govern themselves. Woodrow Wilson discarded Washington's admonition to steer clear of others' nettlesome politics, committing instead to make the world "safe for democracy." The "idea of America," Wilson explained to midshipmen at the U.S. Naval Academy, "is to serve humanity."[5]

Some contemporary commentators believe that we are entering a third act of American foreign policy, one that retains the Founders' skepticism of foreign entanglements but ignores their contention that Americans should be concerned about the global struggle for liberty. Donald Trump has praised numerous dictators, from Egypt's Abdel Fattah el-Sisi to Philippine president Rodrigo Duterte, and he seems generally unconcerned about the plight of oppressed peoples around the world. "All U.S. presidents have, to varying degrees, downplayed or even overlooked concerns about human rights in order to get things done with unsavory foreign partners," notes Sarah Margon of Human Rights Watch. "But none has seemed so eager as Trump to align with autocrats as a matter of course."[6] Contrast such an attitude with John Quincy Adams's famous pledge from July 4, 1821: "Wherever the standard of freedom and Independence has been or shall be unfurled, there will [America's] heart, her benedictions and her prayers be."[7] It isn't clear that Donald Trump's brand of "America First" will endure after he leaves office, but we should be dismayed by the suggestion that free people—or those aspiring to be free—don't deserve at least Americans' sympathy. The question in the modern era is not whether we should aspire to nobler goals than merely protecting and preserving what we have—we emphatically should—but rather how best to confer similar blessings on others. Libertarians want liberty for *all* human beings, not merely those living in the comfortable confines of the United States of America.

The United States can still be a beacon of liberty for others; we can serve as an example for others to follow. If we employ an overly heavy-handed approach, however, we may engender resistance from those jealous to preserve their independence from foreign influences.

Individuals who profess great pride in the wisdom and justice of human liberty as the centerpiece of a good and just society betray a curious lack of confidence in their ideas when they imply that these ideas can only survive under the covering fire of American armaments.

It is true that a U.S. general, Douglas MacArthur, effectively compelled the Japanese to adopt democracy at gunpoint after the devastation of World War II. The United States supported military dictatorships and authoritarians during the course of the Cold War, and some of these dictators did occasionally push policies that were loosely conducive to some elements of liberalism. But accommodating autocracy is hardly the best model for spreading human freedom.

Good governance, which accords citizens a say in how they are governed and respects basic human rights and property rights, has spread organically in the last half century. Freedom has proceeded in fits and starts, but things are improving. People are living better, healthier, more fulfilling lives. Pockets of illiberalism and oppression persist today, but it is becoming harder, not easier, for dictators and autocrats to hold back the tide of history.

In fact, much of this progress has occurred entirely independent of the actions of the U.S. government. U.S. foreign policy, from military intervention to diplomacy to foreign aid, can only touch so many people and places, and it doesn't always advance the cause of liberty. By contrast, countless nongovernmental organizations and charities, from the Bill and Melinda Gates Foundation, to Feed the Children, to Doctors without Borders, have contributed greatly to human betterment, on a scale that not even the mighty United States of America can match.

Put another way, some people say that liberty needs a champion; that's true enough. But it's better yet if there are millions of such men and women who spread the message of individual liberty, limited government, free markets, and peace and who do so independently of any government and without resorting to coercion or the threat of violence.

It is reasonable to doubt that such people can prevail over tyrants determined to retain control at all costs. Syria's Bashar al-Assad was more willing to turn his regime's guns on protesters than was Egypt's Hosni Mubarak. The former is still in power; the other stood trial in a cage in a Cairo courtroom.

Does anyone doubt that Xi Jinping would react any differently than Deng Xiaoping to an uprising on the scale of the Tiananmen protests from over a quarter century ago? Would the House of Saud welcome popular uprisings demanding more rights for women or religious and ethnic minorities? It seems unlikely.

And yet there are moments throughout human history when ordinary people do extraordinary things in the service of freedom, often at great risk to their own life and well-being. In late 2010, Tunisian fruit vendor Mohamed Bouazizi set himself on fire to protest his mistreatment at the hands of Tunisian authorities. The desperate act of defiance precipitated popular uprisings in Libya, Syria, Egypt, Yemen, and Bahrain. These were not the work of the U.S. government. A more satisfying (and accurate) explanation is that these were spontaneous expressions of public sentiment, motivated chiefly by a desire to throw off decades of authoritarian rule.

It shouldn't have taken a disastrous war in Iraq—and a string of other unsatisfying attempts at forcible regime change—to remind Americans why they shouldn't trust the U.S. government to promote human freedom. But if these weren't enough, the presidential election of 2016 should have finished the job.

In November 2016, the American people elected a man who rejected foundational liberal values, including tolerance and respect for human rights. He questioned the worth of free speech and a free press. He challenged the American legal system, including the independence of judges and the loyalty of senior law enforcement agents. The American people elected a man generally ignorant about—and at times openly disdainful of—past U.S. efforts to spread liberty. In short, now is a particularly inauspicious time for the United States to be lecturing others on how to craft a liberal society. We still have work to do here.

But even if Americans could be counted on to always elect to high office men and women committed to classical liberalism, the cause is too important and the planet too large and complex to trust the promotion of liberty to a single country. Not even 320 million Americans all working together to advance principles of freedom and personal autonomy could convince 7 billion people elsewhere to embrace these ideas.

Thankfully, the cause of liberty can and has spread organically, virally, as more and more people see the benefits of living in a free society. As liberty and liberalism slowly penetrate even the most closed and conservative societies, those who chafe at the restrictions that the old order imposes on them struggle even harder to lose the yoke.

Sometimes, they will look to outsiders for help. But often, such assistance breeds disillusionment, resentment, and even anger if reality doesn't live up to their expectations.

The Iraqis who tried to topple Saddam Hussein's statue in April 2003 couldn't finish the job on their own. Not even Kadhim al-Jabbouri, a burly wrestler and weightlifter who swung the sledgehammer with considerable force and determination, could bring it down. He and the other Iraqis then attempted to pull the statue down with ropes, but this too failed.

American troops had supplied those tools but were initially reluctant to perform the deed. They anticipated fierce fighting ahead of them and remained focused for a time on the main task of the day: toppling Hussein's regime, not merely his icon. But once it was clear that Iraqis weren't equipped for the job, the Americans fastened a chain around the hollow bronze statue, hooked it up to an M-88 military tow truck, and ripped the figure to the ground. Elated Iraqis smashed it apart, dragging and carting away the scattered pieces of metal.

Kadhim al-Jabbouri had witnessed the execution of over a dozen family members under Saddam's brutal rule. He had endured more than a year in prison. No one could have doubted his hatred for the old regime. When reporters caught up with him nearly 13 years later, however, he regretted the role he had played in tearing down Saddam's statue. He had longed for peace while Saddam ruled. But after Saddam's fall, as chaos and violence erupted in Iraq, Jabbouri fled with his family to Beirut, Lebanon, one of millions of Iraqi refugees.

"Every year, things started to get worse. There was corruption, infighting, killing, looting," he said. "Saddam has gone, but in his place we now have 1,000 Saddams."

He felt "pain and shame" for having pulled the statue down. "I'd like to put it back up. To rebuild it. But I'm afraid I'd be killed."[8]

No one could doubt the centrality of the role that America played in Iraq. But even ideas and images that—on the surface—appear to take their inspiration from the United States aren't always that way. One of the artists responsible for the Goddess of Democracy statue erected in Tiananmen Square in 1989 explained that they didn't intend for their statue to look like the Statue of Liberty. That would seem too pro-American, he said.[9]

Human freedom, it turns out, springs from many sources. We shouldn't want it any other way.

Acknowledgments

I am grateful to the editors at Libertarianism.org, Aaron Ross Powell and Grant Babcock, for the invitation to write this book, and for their extraordinary patience, as what should have been a one-year project turned into three. Grant also read the entire manuscript and made suggestions for improvement. I also wish to thank my colleagues Ted Galen Carpenter, John Glaser, and Marian Tupy, who read all or major parts of the manuscript at various stages and provided valuable input. I received research help from a number of Cato research assistants and interns, including Jonathan "J.E." Allen, Thasos Athens, Matthew Aquino, Neil Saul, Jake Doddy, Jack Hipkins, Michael Klemencic, James Knupp, Courtney Nadeau, Corinne O'Brien, Anupam Roy, and Connor Ryan; Alice White and Katie Wright helped with copyediting.

Notes

Preface

1. Quoted in Andrew Bacevich, *The Limits of Power: The End of American Exceptionalism* (New York: Henry Holt, 2008), p. 157.

Chapter 1

1. James Madison, "Political Observations" (1795), in *Letters and Other Writings of James Madison: Fourth President of the United States*, ed. Philip R. Fendall (Philadelphia: J. B. Lippincott & Co, 1865), vol. 4, p. 491.

2. Ronald Hamowy, "Peace and Pacifism," in *The Encyclopedia of Libertarianism*, ed. Ronald Hamowy (Los Angeles: Sage, 2008), p. 374.

3. Bruce Porter, *War and the Rise of the State: The Military Foundations of Modern Politics* (New York: The Free Press, 1994), p. xv.

4. Hamowy, "Peace and Pacifism," p. 374.

5. Quoted in Hamowy, p. 374.

6. Quoted in Hamowy, p. 374.

7. Quoted in Carolyn Lochhead, "Friedman's 'Heresy' Hits Mainstream," *San Francisco Chronicle*, June 5, 2005.

8. Porter, *War and the Rise of the State*, p. 280.

9. Robert Higgs, *Crisis and Leviathan: Critical Episodes in the Growth of American Government* (New York: Oxford University Press, 1987).

10. Ivan Eland, "Warfare State to Welfare State: Conflict Causes Government to Expand at Home," *The Independent Review* 18, no. 2 (Fall 2013): 189–218.

11. Quoted in Richard K. Betts, "Suicide from Fear of Death?," *Foreign Affairs*, January/February 2003, p. 35.

12. F. A. Hayek, *The Fatal Conceit: The Errors of Socialism*, ed. W. W. Bartley III (Chicago: University of Chicago Press, 2011), p. 27.

13. David Boaz, *The Libertarian Mind: A Manifesto for Freedom* (New York: Simon and Schuster, 2015), p. 326.

14. Robert Kagan, *The World America Made* (New York: Alfred A. Knopf, 2012), pp. 8–9.

15. Steven Pinker, *The Better Angels of Our Nature: Why Violence Has Declined* (New York: Viking Books, 2011).

Chapter 2

1. Madison, "Political Observations," p. 491.

2. Benjamin Franklin, "From Benjamin Franklin to Josiah Quincy, Sr., 11 September 1783," in *The Papers of Benjamin Franklin*, ed. Ellen R. Cohn (New Haven and London: Yale University Press, 2011), vol. 40, pp. 611–13. Available from the National Archives at https://founders.archives.gov/documents/Franklin/01-40-02-0385.

3. George Washington, "Washington's Farewell Address" (Sept. 17, 1796), Yale Law School's Avalon Project, http://avalon.law.yale.edu/18th_century/washing.asp.

4. Porter, *War and the Rise of the State*, p. 250.

5. "Declaration and Resolves of the First Continental Congress" (Oct. 14, 1774), Yale Law School's Avalon Project, http://avalon.law.yale.edu/18th_century/resolves.asp.

6. James Madison, "Madison Debates" (June 29, 1787), Yale Law School's Avalon Project, http://avalon.law.yale.edu/18th_century/debates_629.asp.

7. James Madison, "Address to the Constitutional Convention" (June 29, 1787), in *Records of the Federal Convention of 1787*, vol. 1, ed. Max Farrand (1911), p. 465.

8. Patrick Henry, "Virginia Ratifying Convention" (June 5, 1788), in *The Debates in the Several State Conventions on the Adoption of the Federal Constitution as Recommended by the General Convention at Philadelphia in 1787*, ed. Jonathan Elliot (New York: Burt Franklin, n.d.), pp. 51–52. Available from the University of Chicago Press at http://press-pubs.uchicago.edu/founders/documents/a1_8_16s10.html.

9. "Ratification of the Constitution by the State of Virginia" (June 26, 1788), in *Documentary History of the Constitution*, vol. 2 (1894), pp. 145–46, 160, 377–85. Available from Yale Law School's Avalon Project at http://avalon.law.yale.edu/18th_century/ratva.asp.

10. James Madison, "Letter of James Madison to Thomas Jefferson" (Apr. 2, 1798), in *The Writings of James Madison*, ed. Gaillard Hunt (New York: G. P. Putnam's Sons, 1900–1910), vol. 6, pp. 312–14. Available from the University of Chicago Press at http://press-pubs.uchicago.edu/founders/documents/a1_8_11s8.html.

11. James Wilson, "Pennsylvania Ratifying Convention" (Dec. 11, 1787), in *Pennsylvania and the Federal Constitution, 1787–1788*, ed. John Bach McMaster and Frederick D. Stone (Lancaster: Published for the Subscribers by the Historical

Society of Pennsylvania, 1888), pp. 414–18. Available from the University of Chicago Press at http://press-pubs.uchicago.edu/founders/documents/v1ch7s17 .html.

12. James Madison, "James Madison, Letters of Helvidius, nos. 1–4" (Aug. 24–Sept. 14, 1793), in *The Writings of James Madison*, ed. Gaillard Hunt (New York: G. P. Putnam's Sons, 1900–1910), vol. 6, pp. 138–77. Available from the University of Chicago Press at http://press-pubs.uchicago.edu/founders/documents/a2_2_2-3s15 .html.

13. Quoted in Gene Healy, *The Cult of the Presidency: America's Dangerous Devotion to Executive Power* (Washington, DC: Cato Institute, 2008), p. 24.

14. Alexander Hamilton, "No. 69: The Real Character of the Executive," in *The Federalist Papers*, ed. Clinton Rossiter (New York: Penguin, 2003), p. 416. Emphasis in the original.

15. Madison, "Letters of Helvidius, nos. 1–4."

16. Washington, "Washington's Farewell Address."

17. Thomas Jefferson, "First Inaugural Address" (Mar. 4, 1801), Yale Law School's Avalon Project, http://avalon.law.yale.edu/19th_century/jefinau1.asp.

18. Quoted in David Boaz, *The Libertarian Reader: Classic and Contemporary Writings from Lao-Tzu to Milton Friedman* (New York: Simon & Schuster, 2015), p. 412.

19. John Quincy Adams, *Address Delivered at the Request of the Committee for Arrangements for Celebrating the Anniversary of Independence, at the City of Washington on the Fourth of July 1821*, https://www.libertarianism.org/essays/address-delivered -request-committee-arrangements-celebrating-anniversary-independence.

20. Adams.

21. Adams.

22. Adams.

23. Adams.

24. James Monroe, "Monroe Doctrine" (Dec. 2, 1823), Yale Law School's Avalon Project, http://avalon.law.yale.edu/19th_century/monroe.asp.

Chapter 3

1. Richard Gamble, *In Search of the City on the Hill: The Making and Unmaking of an American Myth* (London: Bloomsbury, 2012), pp. 3–4, 6–7.

2. Thomas Paine, *Common Sense* (1776; Project Gutenberg, 2008), para. 83, http:// www.gutenberg.org/ebooks/147.

3. Paine, *Common Sense*, para. 161.

4. Richard Immerman, *Empire for Liberty: A History of American Imperialism from Benjamin Franklin to Paul Wolfowitz* (Princeton, NJ: Princeton University Press, 2012), p. 5.

5. Immerman, p. 13.

6. Immerman, p. 13.

7. Quoted in David Mayers, *Dissenting Voices in America's Rise to Power* (New York: Cambridge University Press, 2007), p. 13.

8. Thomas Jefferson, "From Thomas Jefferson to John Breckinridge" (Aug. 12, 1803). Available from the National Archives at https://founders.archives.gov/documents /Jefferson/01-41-02-0139.

9. Mayers, *Dissenting Voices*, p. 15.

10. Mayers, p. 21.

11. George Herring, *From Colony to Superpower: U.S. Foreign Relations since 1776* (New York: Oxford University Press, 2008), p. 194.

12. Abraham Lincoln, "The Perpetuation of Our Political Institutions: Address before the Young Men's Lyceum of Springfield, Illinois" (Jan. 27, 1838), https://www .libertarianism.org/essays/excerpt-perpetuation-our-political-institutions.

13. Daniel Webster, *The Works of Daniel Webster*, 13th ed., vol. 5 (Boston: Little, Brown, 1864), p. 56.

14. Webster, *Works of Daniel Webster*, vol. 5, p. 259.

15. Quoted in Healy, *The Cult of the Presidency*, p. 41.

Chapter 4

1. Quoted in Stephen Kinzer, *The True Flag: Theodore Roosevelt, Mark Twain, and the Birth of American Empire* (New York: Henry Holt, 2017), pp. 23–24.

2. Quoted in Herring, *From Colony to Superpower*, p. 317.

3. Quoted in Robert Merry, *President McKinley: Architect of the American Century* (New York: Simon and Schuster, 2017), p. 251.

4. Quoted in Merry, p. 319.

5. Quoted in Stephen Kinzer, "How Boston Fought the Empire," *Boston Globe*, January 2, 2017.

6. Quoted in Mayers, *Dissenting Voices*, p. 198.

7. Robert Beisner, *Twelve against Empire* (New York: McGraw-Hill, 1968), p. 6.

8. On Reed, see James Grant, *Mr. Speaker! The Life and Times of Thomas B. Reed: The Man Who Broke the Filibuster* (New York: Simon and Schuster, 2011).

9. Mayers, *Dissenting Voices*, p. 193.

10. Quoted in Walter A. McDougall, *Promised Land, Crusader State: The American Encounter with the World since 1776* (New York: Houghton Mifflin, 1997), p. 112. See also Merry, *President McKinley*, p. 334.

11. McDougall, *Promised Land, Crusader State*, p. 112.

12. Quoted in Kinzer, *The True Flag*, p. 156.

13. Quoted in Kinzer, pp. 156–57. See also Mayers, *Dissenting Voices*, p. 94.

14. Quoted in Kinzer, "How Boston Fought the Empire."

15. Quoted in Mayers, *Dissenting Voices*, p. 204.

16. Quoted in Mayers, p. 204.

17. Quoted in Mayers, pp. 200–201.

18. Quoted in Herring, *From Colony to Superpower*, p. 323.

19. Quoted in Mayers, *Dissenting Voices*, p. 202.

20. Quoted in Herring, *From Colony to Superpower*, p. 321.

21. Quoted in Merry, *President McKinley*, p. 368.

22. Quoted in Kinzer, *The True Flag*, p. 137.

23. Herring, *From Colony to Superpower*, p. 328.

24. Quoted in Mayers, *Dissenting Voices*, p. 195.

25. Miller and Cooper quoted in Mayers, pp. 195–96.

26. Quoted in Kinzer, *The True Flag*, p. 84.

27. Quoted in Mayers, *Dissenting Voices*, p. 199.

28. Quoted in Mayers, p. 196.

29. William Graham Sumner, "The Conquest of the United States by Spain," (Jan. 16, 1899), https://www.libertarianism.org/essays/conquest-united-states-spain.

30. Sumner.

31. Quoted in Mayers, *Dissenting Voices*, p. 205.

32. Quoted in Merry, *President McKinley*, pp. 363–64.

33. Merry, p. 367.

34. Quoted in Kinzer, "How Boston Fought the Empire."

35. Quoted in Kinzer, *The True Flag*, p. 223. See also Mayers, *Dissenting Voices*, p. 202.

36. Quoted in Mayers, *Dissenting Voices*, p. 213.

37. Quoted in Herring, *From Colony to Superpower*, p. 335.

38. Quoted in Mayers, *Dissenting Voices*, p. 215.

39. Quoted in McDougall, *Promised Land, Crusader State*, p. 118.

40. Merry, *President McKinley*, p. 365.

41. Mayers, *Dissenting Voices*, pp. 215–16.

Chapter 5

1. Merry, *President McKinley*, p. 371.

2. Quoted in McDougall, *Promised Land, Crusader State*, p. 115.

3. Quoted in McDougall, p. 115.

4. Herring, *From Colony to Superpower*, pp. 391–93.

5. Woodrow Wilson, "Wilson's War Message to Congress" (Apr. 2, 1917), The World War I Document Archive, May 28, 2009, https://wwi.lib.byu.edu/index.php /Wilson%27s_War_Message_to_Congress.

6. Robert Gilpin, *War and Change in International Politics* (Cambridge: Cambridge University Press, 1983), p. 50.

7. Quoted in Edward Rhodes, "Charles Evans Hughes Reconsidered, or: Liberal Isolationism in the New Millennium," in *The Real and the Ideal: Essays on International Relations in Honor of Richard H. Ullman*, ed. Anthony Lake and David Ochmanek (New York: Rowman & Littlefield, 2001), pp. 172–73.

8. Quoted in Rhodes, p. 173.

9. Thomas Hobbes, *Leviathan* (1651; University of Adelaide, 2016), ch. XIII, https:// ebooks.adelaide.edu.au/h/hobbes/thomas/h68l/index.html.

10. Baron de Montesquieu, *The Spirit of Laws* (1748), in Complete Works, vol. 2 (1777), bk. XX, ch. I. Available from the Online Library of Liberty at http://oll.libertyfund .org/titles/montesquieu-complete-works-vol-2-the-spirit-of-laws.

11. Immanuel Kant, "Perpetual Peace" (1795). Quoted in George H. Smith, "Immanuel Kant on War and Peace," Libertarianism.org, June 20, 2016, https://www .libertarianism.org/columns/immanuel-kant-war-peace.

12. "A Cobden Digest on Free Trade," Libertarianism.org, November 5, 2015, https:// www.libertarianism.org/publications/essays/cobden-digest.

13. John Stuart Mill, *Principles of Political Economy with Some of Their Applications to Social Philosophy*, ed. William James Ashley (London: Longmans, Green, 1909, 7th ed.), bk. III, ch. XVII. Available from the Online Library of Liberty at http://oll .libertyfund.org/titles/101.

14. Norman Angell, *The Great Illusion: A Study of the Relation of Military Power in Nations to Their Economic and Social Advantage* (New York: G. P. Putnam's Sons, 1911). See also Erik Gartzke, "Economic Freedom and Peace," in *Economic Freedom of the World: 2005 Annual Report*, ed. James Gwartney and Robert Lawson (Vancouver: Fraser Institute, 2005), pp. 29–44, https://object.cato.org/pubs/efw/efw2005/efw2005-2.pdf.

15. Quoted in Jeffrey Record, *The Specter of Munich: Reconsidering the Lessons of Appeasing Hitler* (Dulles, VA: Potomac Books, 2007).

16. Quoted in Ernest R. May, *"Lessons" of the Past: The Use and Misuse of History in American Foreign Policy* (New York: Oxford University Press, 1973), p. 36.

17. Quoted in May, p. 37.

18. Quoted in May, pp. 50–51.

19. Quoted in May, p. 62.

20. Quoted in May, pp. 81–82.

Chapter 6

1. Dwight D. Eisenhower, "Military-Industrial Complex Speech" (Jan. 17, 1961), Yale Law School's Avalon Project, http://avalon.law.yale.edu/20th_century/eisenhower 001.asp. To listen to the speech, see https://www.libertarianism.org/media/classics -liberty/dwight-d-eisenhower-farewell-address.

2. Harold D. Lasswell, "The Garrison State," *American Journal of Sociology* 46, no. 4 (1941): 455–68.

3. Higgs, *Crisis and Leviathan*, p. 154–55.

4. Higgs, p. 202.

5. Ted Galen Carpenter, *The Captive Press: Foreign Policy Crises and the First Amendment* (Washington, DC: Cato Institute, 1995), p. 19.

6. Carpenter, pp. 26–27.

7. Carpenter, p. 19.

8. Carpenter, p. 28.

9. Quoted in Robert Mann, *A Grand Delusion: America's Descent into Vietnam* (New York: Basic Books, 2002), https://archive.nytimes.com/www.nytimes.com/books /first/m/mann-delusion.html.

10. Quoted in Thomas Wright, *All Measures Short of War: The Contest for the 21st Century and the Future of American Power* (New Haven, CT: Yale University Press, 2017), p. 156. See also Benjamin Schwarz, "Clearer than the Truth," *The Atlantic*, April 2004, https://www.theatlantic.com/magazine/archive/2004/04/clearer-than-the-truth /302928/.

11. Ernest R. May, ed., *American Cold War Strategy: Interpreting NSC 68* (Boston: Bedford Books, 1993), pp. 25, 52.

12. May, p. 46.

13. Aaron Friedberg, *In the Shadow of the Garrison State: America's Anti-Statism and Its Cold War Grand Strategy* (Princeton, NJ: Princeton University Press, 2000), p. 110.

14. On Eisenhower's overall conduct during the Cold War, see Evan Thomas, *Ike's Bluff: President Eisenhower's Secret Battle to Save the World* (New York: Little, Brown and

Company, 2012). See also Fred Greenstein, *The Hidden-Hand Presidency: Eisenhower as Leader* (New York: Basic Books, 1982).

15. Quoted in Campbell Craig, *Destroying the Village: Eisenhower and Thermonuclear War* (New York: Columbia University Press, 1998), p. xiv.

16. Quoted in Thomas M. Nichols, *No Use: Nuclear Weapons and U.S. National Security* (Philadelphia: University of Pennsylvania Press, 2013), p. 91.

17. Dwight D. Eisenhower, "The Chance for Peace" (Apr. 16, 1953), speech delivered before the American Society of Newspaper Editors, https://www.libertarianism .org/essays/chance-peace.

18. Quoted in James Ledbetter, *Unwarranted Influence: Dwight D. Eisenhower and the Military-Industrial Complex* (New Haven, CT: Yale University Press, 2011), p. 24.

19. Quoted in Robert R. Bowie and Richard H. Immerman, *Waging Peace: How Eisenhower Shaped an Enduring Cold War Strategy* (New York: Oxford University Press, 1998), p. 44.

20. Quoted in Christopher A. Preble, *The Power Problem: How American Military Dominance Makes Us Less Safe, Less Prosperous, and Less Free* (Ithaca, NY: Cornell University Press, 2009), p. 75.

21. Dwight David Eisenhower, "Annual Message to the Congress on the State of the Union" (Feb. 2, 1953), http://www.presidency.ucsb.edu/ws/?pid=9829.

22. Quoted in Richard Immerman, "Confessions of an Eisenhower Revisionist: An Agonizing Reappraisal," *Diplomatic History* 14 (Summer 1990): 328.

23. Eisenhower, "Military-Industrial Complex Speech."

24. Eisenhower.

25. John F. Kennedy, "Inaugural Address" (Jan. 20, 1961), The American Presidency Project, http://www.presidency.ucsb.edu/ws/index.php?pid=8032.

26. Military personnel numbers from "Table 7-5: Department of Defense Manpower"; DOD budget as a share of GDP from "Table 7-7: Defense Shares of Economic and Budgetary Aggregates," in *National Defense Budget Estimates for FY 2018* (Washington, DC: Department of Defense), http://comptroller.defense.gov /Portals/45/Documents/defbudget/fy2018/FY18_Green_Book.pdf.

27. Rebecca Thorpe, *The American Warfare State: The Domestic Politics of Military Spending* (Chicago: University of Chicago Press, 2014).

Chapter 7

1. "Welcome to the Project for the New American Century," https://web.archive.org /web/20130112203305/http:/www.newamericancentury.org/.

2. "Statement of Principles," Project for the New American Century, June 3, 1997, https://web.archive.org/web/20130112235337/ http://www.newamericancentury.org/statementofprinciples.htm.

3. "Letter to President Clinton on Iraq" (Jan. 26, 1998), Project for the New American Century, https://web.archive.org/web/20130112203258/ http://www.newamericancentury.org/iraqclintonletter.htm.

4. William Kristol and Robert Kagan, "Bombing Iraq Isn't Enough," *New York Times*, January 30, 1998, http://www.nytimes.com/1998/01/30/opinion/bombing-iraq-isn-t-enough.html; Kristol and Kagan, "A 'Great Victory' for Iraq," *Washington Post*, February 26, 1998, https://www.washingtonpost.com/archive/opinions/1998/02/26/a-great-victory-for-iraq/88ed1956-5c57-498d-a37b-118b224ec94a.

5. "Letter to Newt Gingrich and Trent Lott on Iraq" (May 29, 1998), Project for the New American Century, https://web.archive.org/web/20130109214724/ http://www.newamericancentury.org/iraqletter1998.htm.

6. William J. Clinton, "Statement on Signing the Iraq Liberation Act of 1998," October 31, 1998, http://www.presidency.ucsb.edu/ws/?pid=55205. See also Ted Galen Carpenter, *Gullible Superpower: U.S. Support for Bogus Democratic Movements* (Cato Institute, 2019), pp. 121–22.

7. "Text: Cheney on Bin Laden Tape," *Washington Post*, December 9, 2001, http://www.washingtonpost.com/wp-srv/nation/specials/attacked/transcripts/cheneytext_120901.html.

8. Central Intelligence Agency, "Terrorism Discovery That 11 September 2001 Hijacker Mohammed Atta Did Not Travel to the Czech Republic on 31 May 2000," December 8, 2001, https://www.documentcloud.org/documents/368985-2001-12-08-terrorism-discovery-that-11-september.html.

9. "Bush's War," *Frontline*, PBS, March 8, 2008, https://www.pbs.org/wgbh/pages/frontline/bushswar/etc/script.html.

10. Aram Roston, *The Man Who Pushed America to War: The Extraordinary Life, Adventures, and Obsessions of Ahmad Chalabi* (New York: Nation Books, 2008), p. 196. See also James Bamford, "The Man Who Sold the War," *Rolling Stone*, June 24, 2010; and Carpenter, *Gullible Superpower*, pp. 127–28.

11. "Full Text of Colin Powell's Speech," *The Guardian*, February 5, 2003, https://www.theguardian.com/world/2003/feb/05/iraq.usa. On Curveball, see John Prados, "The Record on Curveball: Declassified Documents and Key Participants Show the Importance of Phony Intelligence in the Origins of the Iraq War," National Security Archive Electronic Briefing Book 234, November 5, 2007, https://nsarchive2.gwu.edu/NSAEBB/NSAEBB234/.

12. John Brennan, interview, *Frontline*, PBS, March 8, 2006, https://www.pbs.org /wgbh/pages/frontline/darkside/interviews/brennan.html.

13. Paul Pillar, interview, *Frontline*, PBS, June 20, 2006, https://www.pbs.org/wgbh /pages/frontline/darkside/interviews/pillar.html.

14. U.S. House of Representatives Committee on Government Reform, Minority Staff, Special Investigation Division, *Iraq on the Record: The Bush Administration's Public Statements on Iraq*, March 16, 2004, http://web.archive.org/web/20060514140012/ http:/www.house.gov/reform/min/pdfs_108_2/pdfs_inves/pdf_admin_iraq_on _the_record_rep.pdf.

15. U.S. Senate Select Committee on Intelligence, *Postwar Findings about Iraq's WMD Programs and Links to Terrorism and How They Compare with Prewar Assessments*, 109th Congress, 2nd Session, September 8, 2006, http://www.emptywheel.net /wp-content/uploads/2013/03/phaseiiaccuracy-1.pdf.

16. Kenneth Pollack, *The Threatening Storm: The Case for Invading Iraq* (New York: Random House, 2002), p. 397.

17. Lawrence F. Kaplan and William Kristol, *The War over Iraq: Saddam's Tyranny and America's Mission* (New York: Henry Holt, 2003).

18. "War with Iraq Is *Not* in America's National Interest," *New York Times*, September 26, 2002, http://www.bear-left.com/archive/2002/0926oped.html.

19. John J. Mearsheimer and Stephen A. Walt, "An Unnecessary War," *Foreign Policy*, January-February 2003, pp. 50–59, available at http://mearsheimer.uchicago.edu /pdfs/A0032.pdf.

20. William A. Niskanen, "U.S. Should Refrain from Attacking Iraq," *Chicago Sun-Times*, December 7, 2001, https://www.cato.org/publications/commentary/us -should-refrain-attacking-iraq.

21. Quoted in Gene Healy, "The Iraq War's Unhappy Anniversary," *Washington Examiner*, May 18, 2013, http://www.washingtonexaminer.com/gene-healy-the-iraq-wars -unhappy-anniversary/article/2524705.

22. Ted Galen Carpenter, "Overthrow Saddam? Be Careful What You Wish For," Cato Commentary, January 14, 2002, https://www.cato.org/publications/commentary /overthrow-saddam-be-careful-what-you-wish.

23. Gene Healy, "The Wrong Place, the Wrong Time, the Wrong War," *Liberty*, January 2003, p. 29.

24. Ivan Eland and Bernard Gourley, "Why the United States Should Not Attack Iraq," Cato Institute Policy Analysis no. 464, December 29, 2002, p. 9.

25. Gordon Lubold, "U.S. Spent $5.6 Trillion on Wars in Middle East and Asia: Study," *Wall Street Journal*, November 8, 2017, https://www.wsj.com/articles/study -estimates-war-costs-at-5-6-trillion-1510106400.

26. See, for example, Gene Healy, "Goodbye, Obama," *Reason*, February 2017, http:// reason.com/archives/2017/01/10/goodbye-obama.

27. On the bin Laden raid, see David Sanger, *Confront and Conceal: Obama's Secret Wars and Surprising Use of American Power* (New York: Penguin Random House, 2013), pp. 88–107.

28. Mark Schoofs, "Coming to an Airport Near You: The Virtual Strip Search," *Wall Street Journal*, February 18, 2010; and "ACLU Backgrounder on Body Scanners and 'Virtual Strip Searches,'" American Civil Liberties Union, https://www.aclu.org /aclu-backgrounder-body-scanners-and-virtual-strip-searches.

29. John Mueller and Mark G. Stewart, "Public Opinion and Counterterrorism Policy," Cato White Paper, February 20, 2018, https://www.cato.org/publications/white -paper/public-opinion-counterterrorism-policy.

30. James Madison, "Letter from James Madison to Thomas Jefferson" (May 13, 1798), in Saul K. Padover, ed., *The Complete Madison: His Basic Writings* (New York: Harper, 1953), p. 258.

31. H. L. Mencken, *A Mencken Chrestomathy* (New York: Knopf, 1954), p. 29.

32. Emanuel quoted in David Boaz, "Obama's Shock Doctrine," Cato at Liberty, November 22, 2008, https://www.cato.org/blog/obamas-shock-doctrine.

Chapter 8

1. Hayek, *The Fatal Conceit*, pp. 27, 71.

2. Otto von Bismarck, *Bismarck: The Man and the Statesman; Being the Reflections and Reminiscences of Otto, Volume 2*, trans. Arthur John Butler (London: Smith, Elder & Company, 1898), pp. 101–2.

3. William Kristol, "We Were Right to Fight in Iraq," *USA Today*, May 20, 2015, https://www.usatoday.com/story/opinion/2015/05/20/iraq-saddam-hussein -obama-bush-william-kristol-editorials-debates/27681429/.

4. Cotton and Rubio quoted in David M. Drucker, "Tom Cotton: We Shouldn't Be Ashamed of the Iraq War," *Washington Examiner*, May 21, 2015, https://www .washingtonexaminer.com/tom-cotton-we-shouldnt-be-ashamed-of-the-iraq-war/ article/2564803.

5. Eliot Cohen, *The Big Stick: The Limits of Soft Power and the Necessity of Military Force* (New York: Basic Books, 2017), p. 59.

6. Quoted in Zachary Roth, "10 Years Later: The Architects of the Iraq War," MSNBC, October 24, 2013, http://www.msnbc.com/msnbc/10-years-later-the -architects-the-iraq-wa.

7. See Sam Rosenfeld and Matthew Yglesias, "The Incompetence Dodge," *The American Prospect*, October 20, 2005, http://prospect.org/article/incompetence-dodge-0.

8. Donald J. Boudreaux, "Unintended Consequences," Libertarianism.org, https:// www.libertarianism.org/media/around-web/unintended-consequences; and Rob Norton, "Unintended Consequences," The Library of Economics and Liberty, https://www.econlib.org/library/Enc/UnintendedConsequences.html.

9. Jack Snyder, *Myths of Empire: Domestic Politics and International Ambition* (Ithaca, NY: Cornell University Press, 1991).

10. See Cass Sunstein, "The Paralyzing Principle," *Regulation* 25 (Winter 2002–2003): 32–37, https://object.cato.org/sites/cato.org/files/serials/files/regulation/2002/12 /v25n4-9.pdf; Cass Sunstein, "Throwing Precaution to the Wind: Why the 'Safe' Choice Can Be Dangerous," *Boston Globe*, July 13, 2008; and Jonathan Adler, "The Problems with Precaution: A Principle without Principle," *The American*, May 25, 2011, http://www.aei.org/publication/the-problems-with-precaution-a-principle -without-principle/.

11. Benjamin H. Friedman, "The Terrible 'Ifs,'" *Regulation* 30 (Winter 2008): 32, https://object.cato.org/sites/cato.org/files/serials/files/regulation/2007/12/v30n4-1 .pdf.

12. Friedman, 34.

13. Ron Suskind, *The One Percent Doctrine: Deep Inside America's Pursuit of Its Enemies Since 9/11* (New York: Simon and Schuster, 2006), p. 62.

14. Friedman, "The Terrible 'Ifs,'" 35.

15. Friedman, 40.

Chapter 9

1. This chapter is adapted from Christopher Preble and William Ruger, "No More of the Same: The Problem With Primacy," War on the Rocks, August 31, 2016, https://warontherocks.com/2016/08/no-more-of-the-same-the-problem-with -primacy/.

2. Elaine Sciolino, "Madeleine Albright's Audition," *New York Times*, September 22, 1996. See also Xenia Wickett, "Why the United States Remains an Indispensable Nation," Chatham House, June 30, 2015, https://www.chathamhouse.org/expert /comment/why-united-states-remains-indispensable-nation.

3. Secretary of State Madeleine K. Albright, interview by Matt Lauer, *Today*, NBC, February 19, 1998.

4. See, for example, Stephen G. Brooks and William C. Wohlforth, *America Abroad: The United States' Global Role in the 21st Century* (New York: Oxford University Press, 2016); Stephen G. Brooks, G. John Ikenberry, and William C. Wohlforth, "Don't Come Home, America: The Case against Retrenchment," *International Security* 37, no. 3 (Winter 2012–2013): 7–51; and Hal Brands, *American Grand Strategy in the Age of Trump* (Washington, DC: Brookings Institution Press, 2018).

5. Samuel Huntington, "Why International Primacy Matters," *International Security* (Spring 1993): 83.

6. Bret Stephens, *America in Retreat: The New Isolationism and the Coming Global Disorder* (London: Penguin Publishing, 2015), p. 231.

7. John Mearsheimer, *The Tragedy of Great Power Politics* (New York: W. W. Norton, 2001), p. 41.

8. Washington, "Washington's Farewell Address."

9. Eric A. Nordlinger, *Isolationism Reconfigured: American Foreign Policy for a New Century* (Princeton, NJ: Princeton University Press, 1995), p. 6.

10. Patrick Porter, "It's Time to Abandon the Global Village Myth," War on the Rocks, January 28, 2014, https://warontherocks.com/2014/01/its-time-to-abandon-the-global-village-myth/.

11. Eugene Gholz, "No Man's Sea: Implications for Theory and Strategy," paper presented at the International Studies Association Annual Meeting, Atlanta, GA, March 17, 2016.

12. See, for example, T. X. Hammes, "Technologies Converge and Power Diffuses: The Evolution of Small, Smart, and Cheap Weapons," Cato Institute Policy Analysis no. 786, January 27, 2016.

13. Stephen G. Brooks, G. John Ikenberry, and William C. Wohlforth, "Lean Forward," *Foreign Affairs*, January-February 2013, https://www.foreignaffairs.com/articles/united-states/2012-11-30/lean-forward.

14. Edwin J. Feulner, Arthur Brooks, and William Kristol, "Peace Doesn't Keep Itself," The Heritage Foundation, October 4, 2010, https://www.heritage.org/defense/commentary/peace-doesnt-keep-itself#.

15. Charles Kindleberger, *The World in Depression, 1929-1939* (Berkeley: University of California Press, 1973).

16. Gary Clyde Hufbauer and Paul L. Grieco, "The Payoff from Globalization," Peterson Institute for International Economics, June 7, 2005, https://piie.com/commentary/op-eds/payoff-globalization.

17. Daniel Drezner, "Bucks for the Bang? Assessing the Economic Returns to Military Primacy," in *A Dangerous World? Threat Perception and U.S. National Security*, ed. Christopher A. Preble and John Mueller (Washington, DC: Cato Institute, 2014), pp. 197, 207.

18. Eugene Gholz, "Assessing the 'Threat' of International Tension to the U.S. Economy," in *A Dangerous World?*, pp. 211–12. On this point, see also Eugene Gholz and Daryl G. Press, "The Effects of Wars on Neutral Countries: Why It Doesn't Pay to Keep the Peace," *Security Studies* 10, no. 4 (Summer 2001): 1–57.

19. Francis J. Gavin, *Gold, Dollars, and Power: The Politics of International Monetary Relations, 1958–1971* (Chapel Hill: University of North Carolina Press, 2004), p. 12.

20. See Michael Mastanduno, "System Maker and Privilege Taker: U.S. Power and the International Political Economy," *World Politics* 61, no. 1 (January 2009): 121–54.

21. Eugene Gholz, Daryl G. Press, and Harvey M. Sapolsky, "Come Home, America: The Strategy of Restraint in the Face of Temptation," *International Security* 21, no. 4 (Spring 1997): 44–45.

22. Benjamin H. Friedman, Brendan Rittenhouse Green, and Justin Logan, "Correspondence: Debating American Engagement: The Future of U.S. Grand Strategy," *International Security* 38, no. 2 (Fall 2013): 191.

23. Robert Jervis, "International Primacy: Is the Game Worth the Candle?" *International Security* 17, no. 4 (Spring 1993): 65.

Chapter 10

1. Washington, "Washington's Farewell Address" (Sept. 17, 1796), Yale Law School's Avalon Project, http://avalon.law.yale.edu/18th_century/washing.asp.

2. Hillary Clinton, "Remarks at FP's 'Transformational Trends' Forum," Foreign Policy Online November 30, 2012, http://foreignpolicy.com/2012/11/30/hillary-clintons-remarks-at-fps-transformational-trends-forum/.

3. This discussion draws from Christopher Preble, *The Power Problem: How American Military Dominance Makes Us Less Safe, Less Prosperous, and Less Free* (Ithaca, NY: Cornell University Press, 2009), pp. 98–99.

4. Mancur Olson, Jr., and Richard Zeckhauser, "An Economic Theory of Alliances," *The Review of Economics and Statistics* 48, no. 3 (August 1966): 266–79.

5. Mancur Olson, Jr., *The Logic of Collective Action: Public Goods and the Theory of Groups* (Cambridge, MA: Harvard University Press, 1971), p. 14, n. 21.

6. Michael Mandelbaum, *The Case for Goliath: How America Acts as the World's Government in the 21st Century* (New York: Public Affairs, 2005), pp. 8–9.

7. Mandelbaum, p. 10.

8. Francis Fukuyama, *America at the Crossroads: Democracy, Power, and the Neoconservative Legacy* (New Haven, CT: Yale University Press, 2007), p. 111.

9. Fukuyama, p. 111.

10. Mandelbaum, *The Case for Goliath*, p. 173.

11. Mandelbaum, pp. 223–24.

12. "The Destruction of USS Maine," Naval History and Heritage Command, https://www.history.navy.mil/browse-by-topic/disasters-and-phenomena/destruction-of-uss-maine.html.

13. Pat Patterson, "The Truth about Tonkin," *Naval History Magazine* 22, no. 1 (February 2008), https://www.usni.org/magazines/navalhistory/2008-02/truth-about-tonkin.

14. Mark Mazzetti and Scott Shane, "Senate Panel Accuses Bush of Iraq Exaggerations," *New York Times*, June 5, 2008, https://www.nytimes.com/2008/06/05/washington/05cnd-intel.html.

15. See, for example, "Global Views 2017," U.S. Public Topline Report, Chicago Council on Global Affairs, August 22, 2017; and Dina Smeltz, Ivo Daalder, Karl Friedhoff, and Craig Kafura, "America Divided: Political Partisanship and U.S. Foreign Policy," Chicago Council Surveys, Chicago Council on Global Affairs, http://www.thechicagocouncil.org/sites/default/files/CCGA_PublicSurvey2015.pdf. In 2015, 38 percent of Americans polled considered "defending our allies' security" to be a "very important" U.S. foreign policy goal; in 2017, that number was 39 percent.

16. "Excerpts from Pentagon's Plan: 'Prevent the Re-Emergence of a New Rival,'" *New York Times*, March 8, 1992, https://www.nytimes.com/1992/03/08/world/excerpts-from-pentagon-s-plan-prevent-the-re-emergence-of-a-new-rival.html.

17. Stephens, *America in Retreat*, p. 102.

18. Barry Posen, *Restraint: A New Foundation for U.S. Grand Strategy* (Ithaca, NY: Cornell University Press, 2014), pp. 44–50.

19. Ian Vásquez and Tanja Porčnik, *The Human Freedom Index 2017: A Global Measurement of Personal, Civil, and Economic Freedom* (Washington, DC: Cato Institute, 2017), p. 10, https://object.cato.org/sites/cato.org/files/human-freedom-index-files/2017-human-freedom-index-2.pdf. Published in 2017 with data from 2015.

20. Among the many excellent sources on the rise of bin Laden and al Qaeda, see Lawrence Wright, *The Looming Tower: Al-Qaeda and the Road to 9/11* (New York: Knopf, 2006); and Steve Coll, *The Bin Ladens: An Arabian Family in the American Century* (New York: Penguin Random House, 2009).

21. Ted Galen Carpenter and Malou Innocent, *Perilous Partners: The Benefits and Pitfalls of America's Alliances with Authoritarian Regimes* (Washington, DC: Cato Institute, 2015), p. 178.

22. Carpenter and Innocent, p. 199. See also Stephen Kinzer, *All The Shah's Men: An American Coup and the Roots of Middle East Terror* (Hoboken, NJ: John Wiley & Sons, 2003).

23. Vásquez and Porčnik, *The Human Freedom Index*, p. 10.

24. Carpenter and Innocent, *Perilous Partners*, p. 390. On the Obama administration's response to Arab Spring uprisings in Egypt, see Sanger, *Confront and Conceal*, pp. 273–367.

25. Carpenter and Innocent, *Perilous Partners*, p. 6.

26. Carpenter and Innocent, p. 6.

Chapter 11

1. Adams, *Address Delivered . . . on the Fourth of July 1821*.

2. John Stuart Mill, "A Few Words on Non-Intervention" (1859), in Michael Doyle, *The Question of Intervention: John Stuart Mill and the Responsibility to Protect* (New Haven, CT: Yale University Press, 2015), pp. 209–10.

3. Mill, pp. 223–24. Emphasis in original.

4. Mill, p. 225.

5. Mill, p. 225.

6. Doyle, *The Question of Intervention*, p. xii.

7. Doyle, p. 14.

8. *Gandhi*, directed by Richard Attenborough (Burbank, CA: RCA/Columbia Pictures Home Video, 1982).

9. Doyle, *The Question of Intervention*, p. 46.

10. Alexander B. Downes and Jonathan Monten, "Forced to Be Free: Why Foreign-Imposed Regime Change Rarely Leads to Democratization," *International Security* 37, no. 4 (Spring 2013): 131.

11. David Edelstein, "Occupational Hazards: Why Military Occupations Succeed or Fail," *International Security* 29, no. 1 (Summer 2004): 49–91.

12. Quoted in Corbett Daly, "Clinton on Qaddafi: 'We Came, We Saw, He Died,'" CBS News, October 20, 2011, https://www.cbsnews.com/news/clinton-on-qaddafi-we-came-we-saw-he-died/.

13. Alan Kuperman, "A Model Humanitarian Intervention? Reassessing NATO's Libya Campaign," *International Security* 38, no. 1 (Summer 2013): 105–36.

14. See, for example, Robert Gates's concerns in Sanger, *Confront and Conceal*, pp. 339–40.

Chapter 12

1. "Military Expenditure (% of GDP)," The World Bank, with data from the Stockholm Peace Research Institute (SIPRI), https://data.worldbank.org/indicator/MS.MIL .XPND.GD.ZS?view=chart.

2. Drezner, "Bucks for the Bang?," p. 203.

3. On this point see, for example, Eugene Gholz and Daryl Press, "Paying to Keep the Peace," *Regulation* 26, no. 1 (Spring 2003): 40–44; and Gholz and Press, "Energy Alarmism: The Myths That Make Americans Worry about Oil," Cato Institute Policy Analysis no. 589, April 5, 2007.

4. Erik Gartzke, "Economic Freedom and Peace," in *Economic Freedom of the World: 2005 Annual Report* (2005), p. 29.

5. Gartzke, pp. 31–32.

6. Gartzke, p. 32.

7. See, for example, Daniel J. Ikenson and Scott Lincicome, "Beyond Exports: A Better Case for Free Trade," Cato Free Trade Bulletin No. 43, January 31, 2011, https:// www.cato.org/publications/free-trade-bulletin/beyond-exports-better-case-free -trade.

8. See the data compiled and curated by the editors at Humanprogress.org, http:// humanprogress.org/.

9. A. Trevor Thrall and Erik Goepner, "Millennials and U.S. Foreign Policy: The Next Generation's Attitudes toward Foreign Policy and War (and Why They Matter)," Cato White Paper, June 16, 2015, https://www.cato.org/publications/white-paper /millennials-us-foreign-policy-next-generations-attitudes-toward-foreign.

Chapter 13

1. This chapter draws from Christopher Preble, *The Power Problem: How American Military Dominance Makes Us Less Safe, Less Prosperous, and Less Free* (Ithaca, NY: Cornell University Press, 2009), pp. 141–44. See also Christopher Preble, "New Rules for U.S. Military Intervention," War on the Rocks, September 20, 2016, https://warontherocks.com/2016/09/new-rules-for-u-s-military-intervention/.

2. On the Powell doctrine and its precursor, the Weinberger doctrine, as useful guides to U.S. foreign policy, see Ian Bremmer, *Superpower: Three Choices for America's Role in the World* (New York: Portfolio/Penguin, 2015), pp. 90–91, 98–99.

3. The original Weinberger doctrine was spelled out in "The Uses of Military Power" (Nov. 28, 1984), speech before the National Press Club, Washington, DC. Reprinted in Caspar W. Weinberger, *Fighting for Peace: Seven Critical Years in the Pentagon* (New York: Warner Books, 1990), pp. 433–48. Quoted text appears on p. 441. Emphasis added.

4. For a criticism, see John Samples, "Congress Surrenders the War Powers: Libya, the United Nations, and the Constitution," Cato Institute Policy Analysis no. 687, October 27, 2011, https://www.cato.org/publications/policy-analysis/congress -surrenders-war-powers-libya-united-nations-constitution.

5. Kenneth Adelman, "Cakewalk in Iraq," *Washington Post*, February 13, 2002, https://www.washingtonpost.com/archive/opinions/2002/02/13/cakewalk-in-iraq /cf09301c-c6c4-4f2e-8268-7c93017f5e93; Paul Blustein, "Wolfowitz Strives to Quell Criticism," *Washington Post*, March 21, 2005, http://www.washingtonpost .com/wp-dyn/articles/A52375-2005Mar20.html.

6. James Madison, "Universal Peace," in *The Writings of James Madison*, ed. Gaillard Hunt (New York: G.P. Putnam's Sons, 1900), vol. 6, http://oll.libertyfund .org/titles/madison-the-writings-vol-6-1790-1802#Madison_1356-06_431.

7. See Daniel Kahneman and Jonathan Renshon, "Why Hawks Win," *Foreign Policy*, October 13, 2009, http://foreignpolicy.com/2009/10/13/why-hawks-win/. Mechanisms for raising the costs of war for American taxpayers, and therefore encouraging a wider debate, include a war surtax, see R. Russell Rumbaugh, "A Tax to Pay for War," *New York Times*, February 10, 2013, http://www.nytimes .com/2013/02/11/opinion/a-tax-to-pay-for-war.html; and market-based veterans insurance, see Michael F. Cannon and Christopher Preble, "The Other Veterans Scandal," *New York Times*, June 15, 2014, https://www.nytimes.com/2014/06/16 /opinion/the-other-veterans-scandal.html.

8. John Yoo, *The Powers of War and Peace: The Constitution and Foreign Affairs after 9/11* (Chicago: University of Chicago Press, 2005), p. x.

Chapter 14

1. Quoted in "A Nation at War; At the Pentagon: 'A Good Day for the Iraqi People,'" *New York Times*, April 10, 2003, http://www.nytimes.com/2003/04/10/world/a -nation-at-war-at-the-pentagon-a-good-day-for-the-iraqi-people.html.

2. Doina Chiacu and Arshad Mohammed, "Leaked Audio Reveals Embarrassing U.S. Exchange on Ukraine, EU," Reuters, February 6, 2014, https://www.reuters.com

/article/us-usa-ukraine-tape/leaked-audio-reveals-embarrassing-u-s-exchange -on-ukraine-eu-idUSBREA1601G20140207.

3. Dov H. Levin, "When the Great Power Gets a Vote: The Effects of Great Power Electoral Interventions on Election Results," *International Studies Quarterly* 60, no. 2 (June 2016): 189–202. See also Levin, "Partisan Electoral Interventions by the Great Powers: Introducing the PEIG Dataset," *Conflict Management and Peace Science*, September 19, 2016.

4. Walter A. McDougall, *Promised Land, Crusader State: The American Encounter with the World since 1776* (New York: Houghton Mifflin, 1997).

5. Quoted in McDougall, p. 131.

6. Sarah Margon, "Giving Up the High Ground: America's Retreat on Human Rights," *Foreign Affairs*, March-April 2018, https://www.foreignaffairs.com/articles/united -states/2018-02-13/giving-high-ground?cid=otr-march_april_2018-021318.

7. Adams, *Address Delivered . . . on the Fourth of July 1821*.

8. Rishi Iyengar, "The Iraqi Guy Who Toppled Saddam Hussein's Statue in 2003 Wants Saddam Back," *Time*, July 6, 2016, http://time.com/4394274/iraq-kadhim -al-jabbouri-saddam-hussein-statue-toppled-baghdad/.

9. Tsao Tsing-yuan, "The Birth of the Goddess of Democracy," in *Popular Protest and Political Culture in Modern China*, ed. Jeffrey N. Wasserstrom and Elizabeth J. Perry (Boulder, CO: Westview Press, 1994), pp. 140–47.

Selected Bibliography and Recommended Readings

Adams, John Quincy. *Address Delivered at the Request of the Committee for Arrangements for Celebrating the Anniversary of Independence, at the City of Washington on the Fourth of July 1821,* https://www.libertarianism.org/essays/address -delivered-request-committee-arrangements-celebrating -anniversary-independence.

Ashford, Emma, Travis Evans, and Christopher Preble, editors. *Our Foreign Policy Choices: Rethinking America's Global Role.* Washington, DC: Cato Institute, 2016.

Bacevich, Andrew. *The Limits of Power: The End of American Exceptionalism.* New York: Henry Holt, 2008.

Bacevich, Andrew. *The New American Militarism: How Americans Are Seduced by War,* Updated Edition. New York: Oxford University Press, 2013.

Boaz, David. *The Libertarian Mind: A Mainifesto for Freedom.* New York: Simon and Schuster, 2015.

Bowie, Robert R., and Richard H. Immerman. *Waging Peace: How Eisenhower Shaped an Enduring Cold War Strategy.* New York: Oxford University Press, 1998.

Bremmer, Ian. *Superpower: Three Choices for America's Role in the World.* New York: Portfolio/Penguin, 2015.

Carpenter, Ted Galen. *The Captive Press: Foreign Policy Crises and the First Amendment.* Washington, DC: Cato Institute, 1995.

Carpenter, Ted Galen. *Gullible Superpower: U.S. Support for Bogus Foreign Democratic Movements.* Washington, DC: Cato Institute, 2019.

Carpenter, Ted Galen. *A Search for Enemies: America's Alliances after the Cold War.* Washington, DC: Cato Institute, 1992.

Carpenter, Ted Galen, and Malou Innocent. *Perilous Partners: The Benefits and Pitfalls of America's Alliances with Authoritarian Regimes.* Washington, DC: Cato Institute, 2015.

"A Cobden Digest on Free Trade." Libertarianism.org, November 5, 2015, https://www.libertarianism.org/publications/essays/cobden-digest.

Downes, Alexander B., and Jonathan Monten. "Forced to be Free: Why Foreign-Imposed Regime Change Rarely Leads to Democratization." *International Security* 37, no. 4 (Spring 2013): 90–131.

Doyle, Michael. *The Question of Intervention: John Stuart Mill and the Responsibility to Protect.* New Haven, CT: Yale University Press, 2015.

Edelstein, David. "Occupational Hazards: Why Military Occupations Succeed or Fail." *International Security* 29, no. 1 (Summer 2004): 49–91.

Eisenhower, Dwight D. "The Chance for Peace" (April 16, 1953). Speech delivered before the American Society of Newspaper Editors. Available at https://www.libertarianism.org/essays/chance-peace.

Eisenhower, Dwight D. "Military-Industrial Complex Speech" (1961). Yale Law School's Avalon Project, http://avalon.law.yale.edu/20th_century/eisenhower001.asp. To listen to the speech, see https://www.libertarianism.org/media/classics-liberty/dwight-d-eisenhower-farewell-address.

Eland, Ivan. "Warfare State to Welfare State: Conflict Causes Government to Expand at Home." *The Independent Review* 18, no. 2 (Fall 2013).

Friedman, Benjamin H. "The Terrible 'Ifs.'" *Regulation* 30 (Winter 2008): 32–40, https://object.cato.org/sites/cato.org/files/serials/files/regulation/2007/12/v30n4-1.pdf.

Fukuyama, Francis. *America at the Crossroads: Democracy, Power, and the Neoconservative Legacy*. New Haven, CT: Yale University Press, 2007.

Gamble, Richard. *In Search of the City on the Hill: The Making and Unmaking of an American Myth*. London: Bloomsbury, 2012.

Gartzke, Erik. "Economic Freedom and Peace." In *Economic Freedom of the World: 2005 Annual Report*, edited by James Gwartney and Robert Lawson, pp. 29–44. Vancouver: Fraser Institute, 2005. Available at https://object.cato.org/pubs/efw/efw2005/efw2005-2.pdf.

Gholz, Eugene, and Daryl G. Press. "Energy Alarmism: The Myths That Make Americans Worry about Oil." Cato Institute Policy Analysis no. 589, April 5, 2007.

Gholz, Eugene, and Daryl G. Press. "Paying to Keep the Peace." *Regulation* 26, no. 1 (Spring 2003): 40–44.

Gholz, Eugene, Daryl G. Press, and Harvey M. Sapolsky. "Come Home, America: The Strategy of Restraint in the Face of Temptation." *International Security* 21, no. 4 (Spring 1997): 5–48.

Greenstein, Fred. *The Hidden-Hand Presidency: Eisenhower as Leader.* New York: Basic Books, 1982.

Hammes, T. X. "Technologies Converge and Power Diffuses: The Evolution of Small, Smart, and Cheap Weapons." Cato Institute Policy Analysis no. 786, January 27, 2016.

Hamowy, Ronald. "Peace and Pacifism." In *The Encyclopedia of Libertarianism*, edited by Ronald Hamowy. Los Angeles: Sage, 2008.

Hayek, F. A. *The Fatal Conceit: The Errors of Socialism*, edited by W. W. Bartley III. Chicago: University of Chicago Press, 2011.

Healy, Gene. *The Cult of the Presidency: America's Dangerous Devotion to Executive Power.* Washington, DC: Cato Institute, 2008.

Herring, George. *From Colony to Superpower: U.S. Foreign Relations since 1776.* New York: Oxford University Press, 2008.

Higgs, Robert. *Crisis and Leviathan: Critical Episodes in the Growth of American Government.* New York: Oxford University Press, 1987.

Ikenson, Daniel J., and Scott Lincicome. "Beyond Exports: A Better Case for Free Trade." Cato Free Trade Bulletin No. 3, January 31, 2011, https://www.cato.org/publications/free -trade-bulletin/beyond-exports-better-case-free-trade.

Immerman, Richard. *Empire for Liberty: A History of American Imperialism from Benjamin Franklin to Paul Wolfowitz.* Princeton, NJ: Princeton University Press, 2012.

Jervis, Robert. "International Primacy: Is the Game Worth the Candle?" *International Security* 17, no. 4 (Spring 1993): 52–67.

Kahneman, Daniel, and Jonathan Renshon. "Why Hawks Win." *Foreign Policy*, October 13, 2009, http://foreignpolicy.com /2009/10/13/why-hawks-win/.

Kinzer, Stephen. *The True Flag: Theodore Roosevelt, Mark Twain, and the Birth of American Empire.* New York: Henry Holt, 2017.

Layne, Christopher. *The Peace of Illusions: American Grand Strategy from 1940 to the Present*. Ithaca, NY: Cornell University Press, 2006.

Ledbetter, James. *Unwarranted Influence: Dwight D. Eisenhower and the Military-Industrial Complex*. New Haven, CT: Yale University Press, 2011.

Lincoln, Abraham. "The Perpetuation of Our Political Institutions" (January 27, 1838). Address before the Young Men's Lyceum of Springfield, Illinois. Available at https://www.libertarianism.org/essays/excerpt-perpetuation-our-political-institutions.

Logan, Justin. "Government, War, and Libertarianism." *Cato Policy Report*, May-June 2008.

Madison, James. "Address to the Constitutional Convention" (June 29, 1787). In *Records of the Federal Convention of 1787*, vol. 1, edited by Max Farrand, 1911.

Madison, James. "James Madison, Letters of Helvidius, nos. 1–4" (August 24–September 14, 1793). In *The Writings of James Madison*, vol. 6, edited by Gaillard Hunt, pp. 138–77. New York: G. P. Putnam's Sons, 1900–1910. Available from the University of Chicago Press at http://press-pubs.uchicago.edu/founders/documents/a2_2_2-3s15.html.

Madison, James. "Letter of James Madison to Thomas Jefferson" (April 2, 1798). In *The Writings of James Madison*, vol. 6, edited by Gaillard Hunt, pp. 312–14. New York: G. P.

Putnam's Sons, 1900–1910. Available from the University of Chicago Press at http://press-pubs.uchicago.edu/founders /documents/a1_8_11s8.html.

Madison, James. "Letter from James Madison to Thomas Jefferson" (May 13, 1798). In *The Complete Madison: His Basic Writings*, edited by Saul K. Padover. New York: Harper, 1953.

Madison, James. "Madison Debates" (June 29, 1787). Yale Law School's Avalon Project, http://avalon.law.yale.edu/18th _century/debates_629.asp.

Madison, James. "Political Observations" (1795). In *Letters and Other Writings of James Madison: Fourth President of the United States*, vol. 4, edited by Philip R. Fendall. Philadelphia: J. B. Lippincott, 1865.

May, Ernest R. *"Lessons" of the Past: The Use and Misuse of History in American Foreign Policy*. New York: Oxford University Press, 1973.

Mayers, David. *Dissenting Voices in America's Rise to Power*. New York: Cambridge University Press, 2007.

McDougall, Walter A. *Promised Land, Crusader State: The American Encounter with the World since 1776*. New York: Houghton Mifflin, 1997.

Mearsheimer, John. *The Tragedy of Great Power Politics*. New York: W. W. Norton, 2001.

Menon, Rajan. *The Conceit of Humanitarian Intervention*. New York: Oxford University Press, 2016.

Mill, John Stuart. "A Few Words on Non-Intervention" (1859). Available at https://www.libertarianism.org/publications /essays/few-words-non-intervention-excerpts.

Mill, John Stuart. *Principles of Political Economy with Some of Their Applications to Social Philosophy*, 7th ed., edited by William James Ashley. London: Longmans, Green, 1909. Available from the Online Library of Liberty at http:// oll.libertyfund.org/titles/101.

Monroe, James. "Monroe Doctrine" (December 2, 1823). Yale Law School's Avalon Project, http://avalon.law.yale.edu /19th_century/monroe.asp.

Mueller, John, and Mark G. Stewart. *Chasing Ghosts: The Policing of Terrorism*. New York: Oxford University Press, 2016.

Nordlinger, Eric A. *Isolationism Reconfigured: American Foreign Policy for a New Century*. Princeton, NJ: Princeton University Press, 1995.

Olson, Mancur. *The Logic of Collective Action: Public Goods and the Theory of Groups*. Cambridge, MA: Harvard University Press, 1971.

Olson, Mancur, and Richard Zeckhauser. "An Economic Theory of Alliances." *The Review of Economics and Statistics* 48, no. 3 (August 1966): 266–79.

Paine, Thomas. *Common Sense* (1776). Project Gutenberg, 2008. Available at http://www.gutenberg.org/ebooks/147.

Pinker, Steven. *The Better Angels of Our Nature: Why Violence Has Declined.* New York: Viking Books, 2011.

Porter, Bruce. *War and the Rise of the State: The Military Foundations of Modern Politics.* New York: The Free Press, 1994.

Porter, Patrick. *The Global Village Myth: Distance, War, and the Limits of Power.* Washington, DC: Georgetown University Press, 2015.

Posen, Barry R. *Restraint: A New Foundation for U.S. Grand Strategy.* Ithaca, NY: Cornell University Press, 2014.

Preble, Christopher A. *The Power Problem: How American Military Dominance Makes Us Less Safe, Less Prosperous, and Less Free.* Ithaca, NY: Cornell University Press, 2009.

Record, Jeffrey. *The Specter of Munich: Reconsidering the Lessons of Appeasing Hitler.* Dulles, VA: Potomac Books, 2007.

Snyder, Jack. *Myths of Empire: Domestic Politics and International Ambition.* Ithaca, NY: Cornell University Press, 1991.

Sumner, William Graham. "The Conquest of the United States by Spain" (January 16, 1899), https://www.libertarianism.org/essays/conquest-united-states-spain.

Sunstein, Cass. "The Paralyzing Principle." *Regulation*, Winter 2002–2003, https://object.cato.org/sites/cato.org/files/serials/files/regulation/2002/12/v25n4-9.pdf.

Thomas, Evan. *Ike's Bluff: President Eisenhower's Secret Battle to Save the World.* New York: Little, Brown, 2012.

Thorpe, Rebecca. *The American Warfare State: The Domestic Politics of Military Spending.* Chicago: University of Chicago Press, 2014.

Thrall, A. Trevor, and Erik Goepner. "Millennials and U.S. Foreign Policy: The Next Generation's Attitudes toward Foreign Policy and War (and Why They Matter)." Cato White Paper, June 16, 2015, https://www.cato.org /publications/white-paper/millennials-us-foreign-policy -next-generations-attitudes-toward-foreign.

Vásquez, Ian, and Tanja Porčnik. *The Human Freedom Index 2017: A Global Measurement of Personal, Civil, and Economic Freedom.* Washington, DC: Cato Institute, 2017. Available at https://object.cato.org/sites/cato.org /files/human-freedom-index-files/2017-human-freedom -index-2.pdf.

Washington, George. "Washington's Farewell Address" (September 17, 1796). Yale Law School's Avalon Project, http:// avalon.law.yale.edu/18th_century/washing.asp.

Wright, Lawrence. *The Looming Tower: Al-Qaeda and the Road to 9/11.* New York: Knopf, 2006.

Index

Pollack, Kenneth 104–105
Porter, Bruce 4–5, 6
Porter, Patrick 135
Posen, Barry 154
postwar economy and Robert
 Higgs 80
Powell, Colin 103, 191
primacy 132–134, 174. *See
 also* foreign policy; global
 power; permanent alliances
 alliances 153–154
 Drezner, Daniel 138
 Gavin, Francis 140
 Gholz, Eugene 139
 Huntington, Samuel 133
 Jervis, Robert 141
 Mearsheimer, John 134
 military costs 133–134,
  139–140
 NATO (North Atlantic Treaty
  Organization) 136
 Nordlinger, Eric 135
 People's Liberation Army 136
 Peterson Institute for
  International
  Economics 138
 Porter, Patrick 135
 Putin, Vladimir 135–136
 technology 134–137
 trade 140–141
 U.S. economy 137–141
prohibition 32
Project for the New American
 Century (PNAC) 100–
 101, 105
Putin, Vladimir 135–136, 196

Qaddafi, Muammar 170

Quezon, Manuel 50

Reid, Richard 110
rights 1–2. *See also* civil rights
 individual 5, 13
 nations 61, 68
 war 4–8
Roosevelt Corollary 61
Roosevelt, Franklin D. 63–64,
 154–155
Roosevelt, Theodore 48–49, 56,
 60, 101
Roston, Aram 103
Rubio, Marco 123
Rumsfeld, Donald 196

Saudi Aramco 155
Sāzemān-e Ettelā'āt va Amniyat-e
 Keshvar (SAVAK) 157
Schurman, Jacob 48–49
September 11. *See* 9/11
Seward, William 41
Shafter, William 48
Shahzad, Faisal 110
Shia Arabs 122
Sisi, Abdel Fattah el- 198
Smith, Adam 5
Snyder, Jack 126–127
Soviet Union 74, 86–88
Spanish-American War 6, 43,
 59–60
 Woodrow Wilson 55
Stalin, Joseph 158
State of the Union address
 (Eisenhower) 91
Stephens, Bret 154
Sumner, William Graham 50–52

About the Author

Christopher A. Preble is the vice president for defense and foreign policy studies at the Cato Institute. He is the author of three books, including *The Power Problem: How American Military Dominance Makes Us Less Safe, Less Prosperous and Less Free* (Cornell University Press, 2009), and has co-edited several other books and monographs, including most recently *Our Foreign Policy Choices: Rethinking America's Global Role* (Cato Institute, 2016), with Emma Ashford and Travis Evans; and *A Dangerous World? Threat Perception and U.S. National Security* (Cato Institute, 2014), with John Mueller.

His work has appeared in major publications including the *New York Times*, the *Washington Post*, the *Los Angeles Times*, the *Financial Times*, *National Review*, *The National Interest*, and *Foreign Policy*, and he is a frequent guest on television and radio.

In addition to his work at Cato, Preble also teaches the U.S. Foreign Policy elective at the University of California, Washington Center, and he co-hosts the War on the Rocks' Net Assessment podcast. He is a member of the Council on Foreign Relations and the International Institute for Strategic Studies.

Before joining Cato in February 2003, he taught history at St. Cloud State University and Temple University. Preble was a commissioned officer in the U.S. Navy, and served aboard the USS *Ticonderoga* (CG-47) from 1990 to 1993.

Preble holds a PhD in history from Temple University.

Libertarianism.org

Liberty. It's a simple idea and the linchpin of a complex system of values and practices: justice, prosperity, responsibility, toleration, cooperation, and peace. Many people believe that liberty is the core political value of modern civilization itself, the one that gives substance and form to all the other values of social life. They're called libertarians.

Libertarianism.org is the Cato Institute's treasury of resources about the theory and history of liberty. The book you're holding is a small part of what Libertarianism.org has to offer. In addition to hosting classic texts by historical libertarian figures and original articles from modern-day thinkers, Libertarianism.org publishes podcasts, videos, online introductory courses, and books on a variety of topics within the libertarian tradition.

Cato Institute

Founded in 1977, the Cato Institute is a public policy research foundation dedicated to broadening the parameters of policy debate to allow consideration of more options that are consistent with the principles of limited government, individual liberty, and peace. To that end, the Institute strives to achieve greater involvement of the intelligent, concerned lay public in questions of policy and the proper role of government.

The Institute is named for *Cato's Letters*, libertarian pamphlets that were widely read in the American Colonies in the early 18th century and played a major role in laying the philosophical foundation for the American Revolution.

Despite the achievement of the nation's Founders, today virtually no aspect of life is free from government encroachment. A pervasive intolerance for individual rights is shown by government's arbitrary intrusions into private economic transactions and its disregard for civil liberties. And while freedom around the globe has notably increased in the past several decades, many countries have moved in the opposite direction, and most governments still do not respect or safe-guard the wide range of civil and economic liberties.

To address those issues, the Cato Institute undertakes an extensive publications program on the complete spectrum of policy issues. Books, monographs, and shorter studies are commissioned to examine the federal budget, Social Security, regulation, military spending, international trade, and myriad other issues. Major policy conferences are held throughout the year, from which papers are published thrice yearly in the *Cato Journal*. The Institute also publishes the quarterly magazine *Regulation*.

In order to maintain its independence, the Cato Institute accepts no government funding. Contributions are received from foundations, corporations, and individuals, and other revenue is generated from the sale of publications. The Institute is a nonprofit, tax-exempt, educational foundation under Section 501(c)3 of the Internal Revenue Code.